FROM LEADING to SUCCEEDING

THE SEVEN ELEMENTS OF EFFECTIVE LEADERSHIP IN EDUCATION

DOUGLAS REEVES

Solution Tree | Press *a division of* Solution Tree

555 North Morton Street
Bloomington, IN 47404
800.733.6786 (toll free) / 812.336.7700
FAX: 812.336.7790

email: info@SolutionTree.com
SolutionTree.com

Visit **go.SolutionTree.com/leadership** to download the free reproducibles in this book.

Printed in the United States of America

20   19   18   17   16   3   4   5

Library of Congress Cataloging-in-Publication Data

Names: Reeves, Douglas B., 1953- author.

Title: From leading to succeeding: the seven elements of effective leadership

   in education / Douglas Reeves.

Description: Bloomington, IN : Solution Tree Press, [2016] | Includes

   bibliographical references and index.

Identifiers: LCCN 2016009094 | ISBN 9781936763917 (perfect bound)

Subjects: LCSH: Educational leadership. | School management and organization.

Classification: LCC LB2806 .R367 2016 | DDC 371.2--dc23 LC record available at http://lccn.loc.gov/2016009094

Solution Tree
Jeffrey C. Jones, CEO
Edmund M. Ackerman, President

Solution Tree Press
President: Douglas M. Rife
Senior Acquisitions Editor: Amy Rubenstein
Managing Production Editor: Caroline Weiss
Senior Production Editor: Christine Hood
Copy Editor: Miranda Addonizio
Proofreader: Evie Madsen
Text and Cover Designer: Abigail Bowen

DEDICATION

For Julie Reeves

ACKNOWLEDGMENTS

My first obligation is to thank the courageous teachers, administrators, and policymakers who have been willing to put their ideas into action. All the research in the world is not as persuasive as the testimony of working educators and leaders who are making these ideas work every day. The hundreds of participants in the Saturday morning #LeadUp chat on Twitter provide a regular supply of ideas, practical experiences, and encouragement. Anyone who thinks that teachers and education leaders have weekends and summers off should see the time that they devote to supporting and encouraging one another and sharing their best ideas on Saturday mornings while juggling family and other professional obligations. Education leaders who have been particularly influential on my thinking in the course of writing this book include David Chojnacki, Lisa Elliot, Chip Kimball, Dennis Peterson, Gabriel Rshaid, and Mike Wasta.

The "References and Resources" section of this book (page 105) is insufficient acknowledgment of the efforts of scholars in this field who tirelessly advocate for courageous leadership. Particularly influential leadership scholars include the late Don Clifton, Linda Darling-Hammond, Richard DuFour, Rebecca DuFour, Bob Eaker, Michael Fullan, James Kouzes, Robert Marzano, Jeffrey Pfeffer, Barry Posner, Tom Rath, and Robert Sutton.

After serving for more than forty years in leadership positions, I understand that some of my most valuable lessons come from my mentors, including the Honorable William Burns, who allowed a young lieutenant to take on responsibilities and opportunities well beyond his abilities. In the course of my daily mistakes with the 144 soldiers under my command, I learned that leadership is defined not merely by our successes but also by the mistakes that we own and from which we learn. After his military service, Bill served in President Ronald Reagan's cabinet as director of the Arms Control and Disarmament Agency, and in the Department of State under Secretary George Shultz. He is a true patriot who inspired a generation of leaders and directly contributed to a generation of peace and the reduction in nuclear arms in the United States and the then-Soviet Union. Since the 1960s, the United States and the world remain deeply divided about the political decisions leading to military action, but there can be no doubt about the commitment of the soldiers and commanders who offer themselves in the United States' hours of need.

Stephen King (2010) quipped that "to write is human, to edit is divine" (p. 16). What makes a book like this come to life is not merely the efforts of the author but also the editing and publishing team that transforms scribbles into some sort of recognizable prose. For that I am deeply indebted to Managing Production Editor Caroline Weiss, Senior Production Editor Christine Hood, Copy Editor Miranda Addonizio, and Proofreader Evie Madsen. I am the husband pacing the floor and looking important as the baby is born, while they are engaged in labor and delivery. Douglas Rife, the president of Solution Tree Press, and Jeff Jones, the chief executive officer of Solution Tree, also know a few things about leadership. Their commitment to a combination of the printed word; 21st century technology; and old-fashioned, face-to-face dialogue represent the best in education, publishing, and professional learning.

While I was working on this book, my mother, Julie Reeves—to whom this book is dedicated—was finishing a longer volume of original research on "Carrie Nation," the latest in her series of historical papers, which includes stories about Abraham Lincoln as a young lawyer before his political career, as well as a host of other challenging and engaging topics. She does this at the age of ninety-four with limited eyesight—feats that makes her sons, including a decorated army general, a business leader and philanthropist, and a teacher, officially lazy miscreants. Did I mention that she also teaches Sunday school, paints murals, and writes an original Christmas play every year? In her sixties, she assumed the presidency of an international arts organization and, throughout my life, I've observed her as a constant leader, laborer, and friend. In sum, the lessons of leadership that I have acquired began early with parents who assumed that women and men not only have the opportunity but the obligation to be effective and selfless leaders. As she marches toward the century mark, Julie's telephone answering machine message says, "This is Julie. I'm busy elsewhere." May it ever be so.

While I am happy to share credit, the blame for errors of commission and omission are mine alone.

Solution Tree Press would like to thank the following reviewers:

Bill Adams
Superintendent
Janesville-Waldorf-Pemberton
    Public Schools
Janesville, Minnesota

Shawn Blankenship
Principal
Piedmont Intermediate School
Piedmont, Oklahoma

Anthony D. Bridgeman
Principal
West Islip High School
West Islip, New York

Tom Colabufo
Principal
Woodland Elementary School
East Syracuse, New York

Diane Goodman
Principal
Cinnabar Valley Elementary School
Nanaimo, British Columbia, Canada

Rick Yee
Principal
Christa McAuliffe School
Saratoga, California

Visit **go.SolutionTree.com/leadership** to download the free reproducibles in this book.

TABLE OF CONTENTS

6 Change 79

7 Sustainability 97

ABOUT THE AUTHOR

Douglas Reeves, PhD, is the founder of Creative Leadership Solutions. He has worked with education, business, nonprofit, and government organizations throughout the world. The author of more than thirty books and more than eighty articles on leadership and organizational effectiveness, he has twice been named to the Harvard University Distinguished Authors Series. Dr. Reeves was named the Brock International Laureate for his contributions to education and received the Distinguished Service Award from the National Association of Secondary School Principals and Parent's Choice Award for his writing for children and parents. He also received the Contribution to the Field Award from the National Staff Development Council (now Learning Forward).

His volunteer work includes free and non-commercial support for doctoral candidates around the world at Finish the Dissertation. He is also the copublisher of *The SNAFU Review*, which contains the essays, stories, poetry, and artwork of veterans recovering from post-traumatic stress disorder. He lives with his family in downtown Boston.

To learn more about Douglas Reeves's work, visit Creative Leadership Solutions (http://creativeleadership.net), or follow him on Twitter @DouglasReeves.

To book Douglas Reeves for professional development, contact pd@SolutionTree.com.

INTRODUCTION

I have about thirty seconds to persuade you that this book is different from the other thousands of books on the subject of leadership, but neither idol worship nor "ten easy steps" can make the critical connection between leadership and impact. What distinguishes this book is *connections*—the links between what leaders *aspire* to do and their actual *accomplishments*. It is not enough for leaders merely to *be*, as leadership descriptions suggest, and it is not enough for leaders merely to *do*. Rather, there are essential *elements* of leadership that represent a combination of who leaders are, what they do, and how they respond to the challenges before them.

The good news is that effective leadership is possible. It isn't the result of an innate set of mystical powers; it is, instead, a result of learning. The bad news is that effective leadership is rare. Annamarie Mann and Jim Harter (2016) of the *Gallup Business Journal* report that the vast majority of people regard their leaders as disengaged, uninformed, uncaring, and incompetent, and only 13 percent of employees worldwide report being fully engaged at work. Most employees would forgo a substantial raise to see their immediate supervisor sent to the gallows . . . or at least exiled from their workplace.

From Leading to Succeeding provides seven elements of leadership that, supported by an international body of evidence, are linked to better performance. But performance is not the typical litany of results, whether measured in quarterly earnings for business leaders or test scores for education leaders. *Leadership* in this context is about the elements that inextricably link leadership to impact.

The inspiration for the structure of this book is the classic text *The Elements of Style* by William Strunk Jr. First published in 1918, the book continues to be a reference for writers, from 21st century bloggers to their ink-stained predecessors. The term *element* is an interesting one, with definitions ranging from the casual, merely a component of the larger body under observation, to the chemical, the basic building blocks of the universe. Human knowledge has progressed a good deal since Aristotle suggested that the world consisted of four basic elements—fire, water, air, and earth.

Similarly, the ancients wrote about leadership, and there remains a good deal to learn by studying older texts, including the Hebrew Bible, the Quran, the Bhagavad Gita, the Christian Gospels, the Magna Carta, the Napoleonic Code, and the Declaration of Independence, to name just a few. While the intervening centuries have taught us a few things about leadership, some thinkers in each era have the conceit that they are the final arbiters of truth.

I make no such pretense. In this respect, I do not take as my model the soaring rhetoric of Gandhi, Churchill, or Franklin D. Roosevelt, but rather their rough drafts. For example, the best part of a tour of the Franklin D. Roosevelt Presidential Library and Museum in Hyde Park, New York, is not the newspaper headlines, the radio fireside chats, or the pictures showing the United States in recovery from the Great Depression and World War II. For me, it is the seldom noticed and underappreciated rough drafts of FDR's most famous speeches, the margins of which contain Roosevelt's handwritten amendments. Only later drafts of the first inaugural address of 1933 contain the phrase "The only thing we have to fear is fear itself," and the same is true of the phrase in his address to a shaken United States eight years later, "A date which will live in infamy."

These phrases, and many others like them, were not the product of an orator or writer who was singularly inspired, but rather of a team that moved and inspired the world. This is an apt metaphor for leadership. It is not the inspired word or exceptional action of a single charismatic person but the work of many, with credit often bestowed on the few. If this book has any value to the leaders who choose to read it, let it be as a reminder to check their egos at the door and remember the many who helped them to achieve their present measure of success.

The seven elements of leadership presented in this book include purpose, trust, focus, leverage, feedback, change, and sustainability. However, agreement with these elements is not essential to provoke important dialogue with colleagues about the nature and purpose of leadership. The book is designed for consumption in bite-sized chunks. For example, each chapter might serve as grist for study and discussion in a leadership meeting or part of a larger discussion within your professional learning community (PLC).

The Elements of Leadership

I present the seven elements of leadership in a deliberate order. Without purpose and trust, the most brilliant execution is without a firm foundation. Without sustainability, the most ardent and well-intentioned leadership efforts will evaporate like the summer's dew. The elements are not a checklist of items to be completed, checked off, and forgotten. Sustainability governs decisions. If a suggestion is not consistent with the stated purpose of an organization, it is abandoned or revised. If an outcome will not or cannot last, we don't invest our time, energy, and resources.

The journey from leading to succeeding requires deliberation. We must allocate time and attention to actions that have the greatest impact on results and fulfill our purpose—now and in the future. If your idea of success is limited to quarterly earnings or annual test scores, then a different leadership book is more likely to meet your needs. If your idea of success is measured in lives changed long after your leadership tasks are completed, then I invite you to continue on this journey.

Purpose

The first element of leadership is purpose. When leaders have a guiding purpose, members of the organization can sometimes forgive them for errors in execution. But without clarity of purpose, cynicism becomes the reigning emotion throughout the entire organization. The enduring success of Scott Adams's (1997) *Dilbert*, the cartoon that embodies organizational cynicism, is a testament to the prevalence of what one of the strip's characters famously calls "process pride." Popular initiatives (strategic planning and standards implementation, for example) often seem to favor elevation of process over purpose.

Before you convene your next meeting, make your next phone call, or write another task on your endless to-do list, ask the fundamental question, What is our purpose? In order to create a purpose-driven organization, leaders must also have deep and abiding passion for that purpose. Passion is what sustains leaders and followers. Passion demonstrates why the purpose is worthwhile and prevents leaders from compromising on the essentials of purpose. Leaders with passion behind their purpose can follow the advice of 17th century theologian Rupertus Meldenius, who wrote (originally in Latin and translated), "In essentials, unity; in nonessentials, liberty; in all things, charity" (Cherok, 2015). Leaders with purpose know the essentials and convey them clearly and consistently throughout the organization without becoming dictators.

Trust

The second element of leadership is trust. According to the American Psychological Association (2014), more than 50 percent of employees distrust their employers, and the level of disengagement among teachers, in particular, is at an all-time high (Riggs, 2013). How did this happen? I've worked with many educational leaders, and I don't know of a single one who aspired to be untrustworthy. Yet an astoundingly high number of them fall victim to the gap between rhetoric and reality. Their speeches at the beginning of the school year about how much they value teachers are quickly eclipsed by the absence of collaboration. Their promises of parental involvement are overshadowed by hierarchical decision making that leaves out a parental perspective. They contradict their commitment to mission and vision with bureaucratic processes that undermine their values. Trust is not about what leaders *say* but rather what they *do*.

Focus

The third element of leadership is focus. Research on more than two thousand school plans reveals that schools with six or fewer priorities experience significantly higher gains in student achievement than the typical school with dozens of strategic priorities (Reeves, 2011). Fragmentation is even worse at the district level, where initiatives become an accumulation of the suggestions of every board member, political leader, grant provider, and teacher leader.

Considered individually, each suggestion has splendid potential. But piled on top of one another, these initiatives divert the energy, time, and money of the entire system. For example, PLCs are one of the most important and influential initiatives since the 1990s. Yet I have witnessed school leaders claim that "we are doing PLCs," only to discover that they simply changed the name of their faculty meeting (DuFour & Reeves, 2016). Rather than the collaborative insights that lie at the heart of PLCs, the frantic, fragmented, and administrator-focused meetings continued as if no one had rearranged the chairs in the faculty meeting for years.

Leverage

How does one decide where to focus? The fourth element of leadership is leverage, a systematic inquiry into the specific leadership actions associated with the greatest improvements in student results and organizational effectiveness.

John Hattie and Gregory C. R. Yates (2014) draw the essential distinction between the question, What works? and the more important question, What works best?

Going by the very low bar of statistical significance, just about anything works—that is, most interventions have a nonrandom relationship to student results. There is a significant research bias in favor of establishing significant relationships. However, scholars can better serve the world of education by honestly writing, "While this initiative might show statistically significant results, it has no practical significance. Time and energy devoted to this initiative would be better diverted to other, more useful efforts."

For example, researchers have established that one of the highest-leverage strategies in education is nonfiction writing (Reeves, 2006a). The Common Core State Standards (CCSS) encourage a significant increase in argumentative writing. This policy prescription is excellent but holds little value if teachers and administrators give it equal weight with everything else in the Common Core. Similarly, effective and accurate feedback has a disproportionate impact on student results. Teachers and administrators following the principle of leverage would therefore devote far more time to nonfiction writing and effective feedback than to other initiatives with less impact. Being statistically significant is not enough. Leverage requires school leaders to systematically analyze the return on investment of the time and resources teachers and education systems expend.

Feedback

The fifth element of leadership is feedback. In no other area is there a greater divergence between evidence and practice. We know what effective feedback looks like—just watch a great music teacher or excellent athletic coach. Every student should receive immediate and specific feedback. Even the most casual observer can draw a relationship between effective feedback and improved performance. But in many classrooms, feedback has been reduced to telling students only if they are right or wrong, without specifics. If the music teacher shouts "Wrong note!" without explaining whether to sing higher or lower, louder or softer, or slower or faster, he or she can hardly expect improvement. Effective feedback depends on specificity.

We evaluate teachers with incomprehensible statistical models and encyclopedic checklists. We evaluate students with assessments that are only distantly linked to daily classroom practice and with grading policies that are inaccurate and unfair. We evaluate leaders at the end of their contracts, long after any coaching might have improved their performance. Leaders who get everything else right but get feedback wrong run into a wall of demoralized opposition.

Change

How can leaders improve trust, focus, leverage, and feedback? They must master the art of leading change, the sixth element of leadership. Change requires leaders to acknowledge that present practices are not working. While many leaders confess their need to change, it is still exceptionally difficult for them to directly answer the questions, What will you change? What is something that you control, over which you have personal influence, that you can do differently today?

Change leadership involves a challenging paradox. While governing boards hire leaders expecting the candidates to be agents of change, they quickly become disenchanted when the leaders do precisely that—engage in difficult but necessary change initiatives. One superintendent I admire very much, a close friend, has repeated this cycle five times: enter as the hero, achieve great results, and exit as the unpopular villain. Change leadership is not popular or a key to career security; it is essential.

Sustainability

The seventh and final element of leadership is sustainability. The best leaders are known not only for what they achieve during their tenure but also for what endures long after they leave. *Julius Caesar* showed us that leadership transitions are tricky. As Shakespeare's rendition of Antony's funeral oration put it: "The evil that men do lives after them; the good is oft interrèd with their bones" (Shakespeare, 3.2.75–76). Despite receiving one of the best funeral orations in the English language, Caesar's vision for Roman glory, and a history of successful conquests, the empire quickly descended into chaos.

Most leadership transitions in education are not quite as dramatic, but they certainly can be brutal, public, and destructive. Once an education system acquires the reputation of destroying its most recent leader, it becomes very difficult for that system to entice the best talent to join the leadership team. When the operating assumption of the new leader is that the ideas, values, and loyalties associated with the prior regime were unforgivably wrong, then today's Caesar quickly becomes tomorrow's Brutus, with the crowd changing its affections within moments.

Am I being overly dramatic? With the average tenure of urban superintendents a little more than three years (Council of Great City Schools, 2014), it is easy for veteran teachers and administrators to become somewhat cynical. The same is true at the building level where principal turnover is rampant. Some of the lucrative Race to the Top grants for schools in need of improvement actually demanded replacement of the principal. The ethic of firing the "bad" principals (a judgment based on their students' low test scores) and replacing them with "good" ones (a judgment based on their students' high test scores) is not burdened with any evidentiary foundation (DuFour, 2015b).

One recent study estimates that the cost of principal turnover exceeds $75,000 per school (Childress, 2014). Thus the central challenge of leadership is not merely change but sustainability. Leaders must concentrate their energy over the course of many years on what matters most and what will continue to matter after they have left their positions. Michael Fullan (2005) warns:

> We need a radically new mind-set for reconciling the seemingly intractable dilemmas fundamental for sustainable reform: top-down versus bottom-up, local and central accountability, informed prescription and informed professional judgment, improvement that keeps being replenished. We need, in other words, to tackle the problem of sustainability head-on. (p. 11)

The Truth About Leadership

Leadership consists of seven essential elements: purpose, trust, focus, leverage, feedback, change, and sustainability. With these elements, leaders and those they serve can meet any challenge. But miss even a single one of these essentials, and the efforts of even the most earnest leaders are far less likely to be effective.

The following pages reflect not only the best 21st century research on leadership but also classic literature in the field. While my own forty years of experience in leadership positions certainly influence my writing, I have attempted to bolster every conclusion not with my personal experiences but with contemporary evidence. Although the book is designed for education leaders, we can draw lessons from nonprofit, government, business, and community leaders. Similarly, leaders in other domains have a great opportunity to learn from effective education leaders. This book does not provide a simplistic recipe for success but rather a model for reflection, self-assessment, and continuous improvement. I do not pretend to offer the last word on the subject but, instead, provide a framework leaders can use to synthesize their own experiences, past research, future experiences, and new research.

This book provides a synthesis of the best research on leadership, not elevating one researcher over another, but instead seeking the intersection of many different research methods and perspectives. Thus, we will consider large-scale international databases, case studies, qualitative investigations, quantitative analyses, meta-analyses, and syntheses of meta-analyses.

When a variety of perspectives and methods come to the same conclusion, they approach the truth about leadership. It means learning from mistakes, not just telling war stories that demonstrate miraculously successful decisions. Therefore, this book offers a variety of perspectives from many research methods and a counterpoint to opinions and personal journeys that masquerade as evidence based.

In the ocean of ink spilled about leadership (at this writing, Amazon offers 119,361 titles on the subject), there is an evident zeal to proclaim new, exciting, and contemporary ideas on the subject. This book takes a contrary approach. The essential question is not *What's new?* but rather *What endures?* Although this book presents contemporary evidence on effective leadership, it is also important to consider the enduring evidence on leadership. For example, while technology, globalization, and intense political pressures have in some ways changed the demands placed on leaders, trust and credibility have remained constant over the years.

Jim Kouzes and Barry Posner (2011) report that results from surveys administered to over one hundred thousand people from around world reveal the following:

- Credible leaders are at their best when they are passionate about what they are doing. (p. 173)

- Credible leaders share information. People can't be expected to learn if they aren't given opportunities to make mistakes. (p. 131)

- Shared values can only be sustained through reinforcements built into everyday organizational policies, systems, and programs. (p. 110)

- Credible leaders demonstrate their trustworthiness by acting in the best interests of others. (p. 83)

- DWWSWWD (Do what we say we will do) is what distinguishes leader credibility from personal credibility. Leaders represent their organizations, not just themselves. Leaders' actions must be consistent with the shared values of their organizations. (p. 41)

- Credibility is earned by daily actions leaders take over time. It does not come automatically with the job or the title. (p. 21)

Although credibility is important for a leader, it is an insufficient quality for leadership. Effective leaders require a combination of skills and characteristics that I am calling the *elements of leadership*. It is likely that readers will want to add to the list of seven elements based on their personal experiences and investigations. I welcome such engagement and creativity. However, it is unlikely that any part of this list of seven elements can be eliminated. I have seen many leaders who excel in many respects, but their enthusiasm for every passing opportunity, for example, causes them to lose focus (see chapter 3, page 31). The revolving door of senior leaders suggests that many of these exceptionally qualified professionals offer extraordinary purpose and passion for their education systems, but their ideas lack the sustainability (see chapter 7, page 97) to endure. Add to the elements of leadership as you wish, but omit them at your peril.

The Problem With Best Practices

Although much of the leadership literature focuses on best practices, this approach harbors an inherent deficiency. Stories about best practices are selective, presuming a causal relationship between a leadership practice and exceptional results. They possess a seductive appeal, as leaders apply one best practice, and then another, and then another. Soon, their fragmented efforts undermine promising initiatives and squander the time, attention, and resources of other leaders and organizations. Therefore, we should also consider worst practices.

The world does not need another book telling leaders what to do. What it needs is clear and specific guidance on how to tell the difference between best and worst practices. Even the best practices can become worst practices if leaders implement them inadequately, or they do not relate to improvements in student achievement. Therefore, for each of the seven elements of leadership, I will consider its polar opposite and, along the way, challenge some of the prevailing myths of leadership. It is meaningless to talk about focus without addressing fragmentation. Bromides about trust are of little help without understanding the causes of mistrust. To put a fine point on it, best practices aren't all they are cracked up to be unless we are candid about worst practices.

The other challenge with best practices is the *post hoc* fallacy—that is, presuming that since one event precedes another, the first must have caused the second. By such logic, Napoleon's early victories led him to the disastrous march to Moscow and, inevitably, to Waterloo. The 20th century fascination with measuring industrial processes led to an industry based on high-stakes standardized testing in the 21st century.

Twenty-first century educational Taylorists assume a direct correlation between a reduction in the time required for test preparation (the "raw materials" of student achievement) and test scores (the "finished product" of contemporary accountability measures). This follows Frederick Taylor's 1800s-era belief that there was a direct correlation between reducing the time a laborer hauled raw materials to the assembly line and industrial efficiency. He thought it could be measured in finished products.

This pattern of decisions, incredibly, continues even after researchers have proven it counterproductive (Darling-Hammond, 2015; DuFour, 2015a). In the years ahead, we must be mindful of the dangers of seeing today's challenges through the lens of yesterday's best practices.

Finally, I would like to share a word about hope for leaders and those aspiring to become leaders. There is no formula to protect you from frustration, exhaustion, and occasional fits of despair. These are part of the burden of leadership in any situation, particularly for contemporary education leaders. The antidote is not wishful thinking about changes in public attitudes and national policy—these move slowly, and leaders must answer in the present. The antidote is hope. Hendrie Weisinger and J. P. Pawliw-Fry (2015) report:

> Adults and children who score higher in hope (1) score higher satisfaction, self-esteem, optimism, meaning in life, and happiness; (2) cope better with injuries, diseases, and physical pain; (3) excel in academics from elementary to graduate school; and (4) perform better in sports. What is especially compelling about the last two findings is that they occurred at levels well beyond what the researchers would have predicted based on natural abilities. In other words, hope predicted academic performance better than intelligence, and athletic performance more accurately than natural ability. (p. 236)

This book offers seven elements of effective leadership. Consider reflecting on one element each day of the week, ending your week with a reflection on sustainability. What will endure after you are gone? Stephen Covey (1989) suggests that we write our own eulogies. That's good advice. What endures? I doubt you want someone to utter at your memorial service, "She completed more than 80 percent of the goals of her strategic plan!" The purposes that guide our lives should influence not only our own actions but also the generations to come. Each of the following chapters explores an element of leadership in detail and invites you to have a conversation about what matters most for a leader—you—and an organization. You will finish this book with a sharper focus, greater clarity, and the means to sustain your ideals.

CHAPTER 1

PURPOSE

This chapter explores the first element of leadership—purpose. Traditional methods of expressing the purpose of an organization often yield weak mission and vision statements that suffer from two fatal flaws. First, they don't mean anything; and second, even if they did, no one knows what the mission and vision statements say. But all is not lost. Leaders can and must define their purpose, and they do not need to convene a committee to do so.

Definition of Purpose

Even if you already have institutionalized a mission and vision, I would challenge you and every other leader and educator to have a clearer sense of purpose than school and district mission and vision statements typically express. We not only must answer the question, What do we aspire to be and to do? but also, Why are we here, and what makes us come to school every day? Particularly, leaders must ask, What are we *passionate* about? Defining purpose only in terms of an education mission and vision is cynical in the extreme, especially if we are unwilling to admit that part of it is to create meaningful career opportunities for employees and families who invest a portion of their earnings in taxes that support our communities.

Passion—emotional engagement—and purpose are deeply intertwined. Few people will be passionate about a 5 percent increase in test scores, but nearly everyone can be passionate about saving the lives of students and the future of our communities.

Despite the urge to quantify student results, there is a difference between a score and the emotional engagement that ignites the passion of educators, students, parents, and communities. For example, a gain in scores may or may not be proficient, but a reduction in the dropout rate has a profound impact on a community. For every high school dropout avoided, communities gain in revenues—sales and property taxes, income taxes, housing and automobile sales, and so on—and avoid costs in social services, medical care, community policing, and incarceration (Alliance for Excellent Education, n.d.b).

Rather than ask about what your purpose should be, consider asking what you are passionate about. Can you express your passion and purpose in a few words with absolute clarity? Although the expression of purpose may begin with official statements, such as missions and visions, the ultimate proof is in what leaders and people in the organizations that they lead actually do.

This chapter concludes with a discussion of what to do when purposes are unclear and what path to take when purposes collide. Even the simple phrase *serving stakeholders* is fraught with conflict, as the interests in which students, parents, educators, business groups, taxpayer groups, political officials, and other stakeholders passionately believe may present different solutions for the same challenge. The essential question is not how leaders can satisfy every constituency but rather how they can best serve their ultimate purpose.

The Illusions of Mission and Vision

As timeliness and specificity are crucial elements of feedback, mission and vision are inextricable from purpose. Mission and vision explain your goals and your values, and ultimately, guide your plans for the future. Strategic plans—which typically include mission and vision statements, followed by strategies, objectives, and action plans—have become a fixture of education systems and other organizations around the world. Many mission and vision statements, however, are neither strategic nor are they plans in any meaningful sense of the word. *Strategy*, the *Oxford English Dictionary* (University of Oxford, 2002) tells us, comes from the Greek *strategia*, or generalship. One of the many definitions of the term is "the art or skill of careful planning towards an advantage or desired end" (p. 3055).

Some exceptional strategic plans appear on a single page. The Freeport, Illinois, school district successfully used this technique, with each one-page plan including only four areas of focus: student performance, human resources, partnerships, and equity (Reeves, 2009a). Such brevity is a rare exception; many more strategic plans run into the dozens or even hundreds of pages.

The methodology behind many strategic planning processes explains this profusion of objectives. In the name of inclusiveness, leaders gather teams for strategy sessions, in which they brainstorm a variety of ideas for improving their local school systems. Without realizing the irony, they discuss the merits of 21st century skills and the need for a technology-rich environment, all while using butcher paper on the walls, handwritten notes, and adhesive dots to indicate their support for one idea or another. They transcribe these ideas; sort them into strategies, objectives, and action requirements; and then present the results as a plan. With such widespread community support for the document, dissenters find it difficult to observe that the strategic planning "emperor" has no clothes. I have hardly ever heard a district-level leader or board member say, "Wait a minute, we only have the time and resources to focus on about half a dozen of these objectives. Let's cut the following action items . . . even though they may be very popular with the strategic planning committees."

The strategic planning process typically begins with establishing a mission and a vision. Who could argue with the wisdom of having a mission and a vision? Few people do, since many have no idea what the mission and vision of their school or system actually is. Small wonder. A study by Top Nonprofits (n.d.) examined the best mission and vision statements of high-performing organizations. Their general findings include the following:

▸ The best mission statements are clear, memorable, and concise.

▸ The average length for the top fifty organizations is only 15.3 words.

▸ The average length for the top twenty organizations is only 9.5 words.

▸ The shortest contains only two words.

▸ The longest contains 235 words.

Some examples of top mission statements include the following:

▸ TED: Spreading ideas

▸ USO: Lifting the spirits of America's troops and their families

▸ The Humane Society: Celebrating animals, controlling cruelty

Compare this brevity and clarity with the following mission statement, which paraphrases some of the many that litter the landscape of well-intentioned planning documents of educational organizations.

> Mission: The focus of the educational process should be on student learning and raising the expectations and standards of academic achievement for all students. Our curriculum and instruction should give students the opportunity to reach their full potential and personal goals, provide for their individual differences and interests, and guide them in selecting meaningful academic and career choices. Technology is essential for the preparation of lifelong learners as students move into a globally connected society. The district should provide an excellent faculty, administration, and support staff who utilize the resources of the community to fulfill its vision. The district shares accountability of an excellent education with students, parents, and the community to seek educational excellence. The district should provide facilities that are designed to enhance the educational process.

It is ponderous and hardly unique to K–12 education. Kevin Kiley (2011) discovered that university and college mission statements routinely consisted of hundreds of words that sought to placate everyone while communicating with no one.

Corporations, nonprofit organizations, governmental entities, and educational institutions have all fallen prey to the same temptation to create missions that seek to reflect the work of their committees of authors but reflect little of the values that an effective mission statement should convey. They essentially say that diversity is good, inclusion is good, and so are quality, service, integrity, and a host of other desirable attributes. But without the clarity, specificity, and brevity of an effective mission statement, we will never know what these organizations really stand for.

They all mean well, but these organizations simply don't have a chance of translating their missions and visions into the daily activities of staff members. Although no one can challenge the nobility of these ideas, it's difficult to imagine fitting this onto a business card or expecting anyone in the school system to recite it.

After reviewing many mission and vision statements from education, business, and nonprofit organizations, I found the vast majority to be banal and rather uninspiring. Richard DuFour (2015a) offers a tongue-in-cheek automatic "mission statement generator" that might save a lot of time in strategic planning meetings. He calls it the *universal mission statement.*

> It is the mission of our school to help each and every child realize his or her potential and become a responsible and productive citizen and a life-long learner who is able to use technology effectively and who appreciates the multicultural society in which we live as we prepare for the global challenges of the 21st century. (p. 102)

Richard DuFour, Rebecca DuFour, and Robert Eaker (2008) suggest that if mission statements reflected the belief systems present in some schools, they might read as follows:

- "It is our mission to help kids learn *if* they are conscientious, responsible, attentive, developmentally ready, fluent in English, and come from homes with concerned parents who take an interest in their education."

- "Our mission is to create a school with an unrelenting focus on learning; failure is not an option. But, ultimately it will be the responsibility of the student and his or her parents to take advantage of the opportunities for learning." (page 114)

- "Our mission is to take credit for the accomplishments of our highest-achieving students and to assign blame for low performance to others."

- "It is our mission to ensure the comfort and convenience of the adults in our organization. In order to promote this mission, we place a higher value on individual autonomy than we do in ensuring that all students learn. We will avoid any change or conversation that might create anxiety or discomfort or infringe on individual autonomy." (p. 115)

When employed appropriately, a mission and vision can be a compelling statement of what the organization does and what it aspires to become. For example, consider the mission and vision for Santa Fe Community College (n.d.).

Mission: Empower Students, Strengthen Community.

Vision: SFCC is a recognized leader in fulfilling its community's dreams, one student at a time.

It is possible to use this mission statement as a filter for proposed strategies or initiatives. Does it empower students? Does it strengthen the community? A similarly focused mission comes from the Boston Philharmonic: "Passionate music making without boundaries." In its history, the Boston Philharmonic has systematically removed boundaries for audience members, musicians, and composers (Zander & Zander, 2000). Conductor Ben Zander made an incisive comment on leadership when he wrote, "The conductor of the orchestra doesn't make a sound. His picture may appear on the cover of the CD in various dramatic poses, but his true power derives from his ability to make others powerful" (Zander & Zander, 2000, p. 68).

A concise mission statement might read, "Everyone learns every day." A vision statement might be a real vision—one without words—that schools could communicate to stakeholders in communities where fifty different languages are spoken but with a common community commitment to educational success. Rather than the typical "All students will . . . ," a vision statement might be a photo of a diverse group of students wearing graduation caps and gowns. If words are necessary, then perhaps circumscribe the photo with the word *all* in a dozen languages.

"Culture eats strategy for breakfast" is a quote often attributed to management guru Peter Drucker (Favaro, 2014). Regardless of who said it, organizations ignore its warning—elevating strategy over culture. Nowhere is this more evident than in the glorification of 21st century skills in the strategy documents of school systems.

The challenges of bad strategy and unfocused vision are hardly limited to education. In a survey of more than twenty-four hundred senior business leaders, Jon Katzenbach and Paul Leinwand (2015) reported the following:

▸ More than half of the respondents do not believe that they have a winning strategy.

▸ Two out of three companies admit that they don't have the capabilities they need to create value in the marketplace.

▸ Only one in five are fully confident they have a right to win.

▸ The vast majority agrees that they're chasing far too many opportunities.

Among the corporations with declining stature that have nearly incomprehensive mission statements are Avon, McDonald's, and Barnes & Noble. The latter doesn't advance its case by including the following two contradictory statements: "Our mission is to operate the best specialty retail business in America, regardless of the product we sell," and "To say that our mission exists independent of the product we sell is to demean the importance and the distinction of being booksellers" (Zetlin, 2013). Committees that develop mission and vision statements appear much better at adding words to a document than subtracting them.

The Vision Gap

It is not surprising that hopelessly obscure vision statements don't make their way into the hearts and minds of employees. It takes a person of enormous optimism to become a teacher and persevere in the profession. But the level of satisfaction among teachers is suffering, largely in response to a loss of professional autonomy. *The MetLife Survey of the American Teacher* (MetLife, 2013) concludes:

> Principal and teacher job satisfaction is declining. Principals' satisfaction with their jobs in the public schools has decreased nine percentage points since it was last measured in 2008. In that same period, teacher satisfaction has dropped precipitously by 23 percentage points, including a five-point decrease in the last year, to the lowest level it has been in the survey in 25 years. A majority of teachers report that they feel under great stress at least several days a week, a significant increase from 1985 when this was last measured. (p. 4)

There is also a gap between what adults and students in education systems believe, particularly with regard to the impact of work on their future results. Teachers and leaders receive a steady stream of evidence supporting the impact of grit, perseverance, and resilience (Dweck, 2006; Tough, 2012); students can listen attentively while authoritative adults speak, but their personal views reveal a starkly different reality.

In a deeply disturbing survey, Sherri Turner and Julia Conkel Ziebell (2011) report that only 24 percent of inner-city adolescents agree with the statement, "Success is related to effort," while 70 percent disagree. Only 18 percent of the same students agree with the statement, "It's important to be flexible and adaptable," while 79 percent disagree. It is possible that some of this adolescent cynicism is the result of the boring and unchallenging lives that they lead in school.

There is not an education system on earth with a goal to bore its students, but evidence from large-scale quantitative studies reveals that more than three-quarters of secondary school students are unchallenged, disengaged, and bored out of their minds (Turner & Ziebell, 2011).

Ethan Yazzie-Mintz (2010) reports that the High School Study of Student Engagement (HSSSE) 2009 survey reveals four common student perceptions about their schools and school leadership.

1. The school's public image is more important than the students.

2. Adults do not respect students.

3. Adults say one thing and do another, especially when it comes to students.

4. Students' thoughts and feelings don't matter very much.

Yazzie-Mintz continues:

> The primary reasons that students report being bored are that the material wasn't interesting (81%), that it wasn't relevant (42%), and that they had no interaction with their teachers (35%). One-fifth of the students (21%) have considered dropping out of school either "once or twice" or "many times." Of those students, the major reasons that they considered dropping out were: "I didn't like the school" (50%), "I didn't see the value in the work I was being asked to do" (42%), and "I didn't like the teachers" (39%). (p. 56)

Teachers and administrators don't intend it to be this way, but those courageous enough to walk a few miles in their students' shoes find that reality varies greatly from their aspirations of an engaging school day. Alexis Wiggins, an instructional coach at an international school, wrote of her experience in taking the tests she was used to giving:

> Of course it feels ridiculous to have to explain the same thing five times, but suddenly, when I was the one taking the tests, I was stressed. I was anxious. I had questions. And if the person teaching answered those questions by rolling their eyes at me, I would never want to ask another question again. I feel a great deal more empathy for students after shadowing, and I realize that sarcasm, impatience, and annoyance are a way of creating a barrier between me and them. They do not help learning. (A. Wiggins, personal communication, August 5, 2015)

Although this viral post (which has more than half a million hits and hundreds of comments) received some praise for its courage and honesty, others criticized it for being anti-teacher. If we cannot make accurate observations about instruction and leadership, we will never advance the quality of learning in schools. If you would like to try this kind of exercise, see the "Shadow a Student" activity in the appendix (page 101).

Although the high school graduation rate hit an all-time high in 2015 at more than 80 percent, there are still more than five thousand students who drop out of high school every day (Alliance for Excellent Education, n.d.a). This has devastating economic consequences not only for the dropouts and their families but taxpayers as well.

When Purposes Collide

Purposes are sometimes mutually exclusive. It is not possible, for example, for an education system to claim that teaching and leadership are the primary influences on student achievement and then fail to measure teaching and leadership effectiveness and student achievement reliably and meaningfully.

Furthermore, it is not possible to commit a system to an academic goal, such as "Every child will read at or above grade level," as measured by state tests, and also commit to trusting the judgment of each teacher and principal on the most effective instructional methods. The plain fact is that some methods of literacy instruction and school leadership are more effective than others, and an education system unwilling to embrace the best available evidence on effective teaching and leadership will not achieve its academic goals by relying on test scores.

On the other hand, it might be perfectly reasonable for an education system to resist the trends of 2001 to 2016 for the inappropriate use of test scores or, for that matter, to resist external tests of any kind. But those systems must then be honest about their purpose and forego the language of *top ten measureable improvements in achievement* or even *closing the equity gap*. Purpose without accountability creates the same muddle as the overwritten mission and vision statements we have already examined.

Strategic plans often lack focus, accumulating goals and objectives from a wide variety of sources, supposedly to ensure that everyone in the process feels included. The result could be a document longer than the Bible and considerably more difficult to read than the original Hebrew, Greek, and Aramaic. Strategy expert Michael Porter (1996) reminds us, however, that the essence of strategy is choosing what *not* to do. In your next meeting, take a look at your top priorities and then add an explicit statement beginning with the words, "Therefore, we will *not* . . . ."

For example:

"We are committed to teacher collaboration; therefore, we will *not* implement new programs that take place during our currently planned collaboration time in our professional learning communities."

"We are committed to success in literacy; therefore, we will *not* implement additional programs that infringe on the time we have already committed to reading and writing."

"We are committed to fostering a creative environment for students and teachers; therefore, we will *not* implement grading and evaluation systems that punish experimentation and error."

Colliding purposes may be born of good intentions, but they leave a legacy of confusion. Every decision to pursue one goal is an implicit decision to avoid another. When multiple conflicting purposes are piled on top of one another, an organization winds up with no purpose at all. As the Mad Hatter told Alice in Wonderland, if you don't know where you are going, then any road will take you there (Carroll, 1865).

This chapter discussed purpose, the first element of leadership. If you can't recite your mission and vision statements from memory, I hope that this chapter inspires you to reexamine and compare them to those effective statements that explicitly communicate purpose and values. Even the compelling statements of purpose, however, will have no value without the second element—trust. This is the subject of the next chapter.

CHAPTER 2

TRUST

Leaders can be forgiven for many mistakes as long as their colleagues trust them. But a breach of trust, in matters large and small, can devastate the ability of leaders to collaborate effectively with colleagues and execute the plans necessary for success. Leaders must follow a higher standard in terms of both professional and personal relationships. Both come down to the simple maxim of doing what you say you will do. For example, if you promise to give teachers time to learn new standards, create new assessments, review data, and respond to individual student needs, then you cannot consume that time with unnecessary staff meetings or meandering conversations. If you promise to give teachers the opportunity to visit one another's classrooms but cut the budget for substitute teachers, then you need to be willing to take over some classrooms yourself in order to fulfill your promise.

The same is true of trust in personal relationships. If you make promises to your family about the time you will spend with them on weekends, then you can't take home a briefcase full of overdue paperwork. A scene in the movie *Give 'Em Hell, Harry!* (Gallu & Bolte, 1970) brings the audience to its feet. President Truman is writing a letter to his daughter, Margaret, in the Oval Office. After signing the letter and sealing the envelope, he reaches for his wallet to pull out a three-cent postage stamp. We could probably forgive the leader of the free world for using government postage to send a letter to his daughter, but Harry Truman knew that trust was not only about what someone does when the world is watching. It doesn't matter if it's three cents or billions of dollars—trust matters.

The element of trust requires vulnerability. You will miss deadlines, you will fail in meeting some commitments, and you will, however unintentionally, break promises. While many leaders offer excuses about being overwhelmed and stressed, the leader who successfully builds trust quickly and humbly acknowledges the mistakes and asks for forgiveness. These words are difficult but essential: "I know that I made this commitment. I didn't keep it, and I am deeply sorry. Please forgive me."

Distrust and Destruction

It is difficult to overestimate the degree of destruction to teacher morale and professional confidence that distrust can cause. Fullan (2011) explains that some drivers are wrong for whole-system reform. It is not just that these drivers are ineffective, Fullan argues, they actually make things worse. Each of the wrong drivers undermines trust between teachers and other stakeholders and education leaders. Fullan's wrong drivers include the following:

- Giving rewards and punishments rather than capacity building
- Promoting individual rather than group solutions
- Elevating technology investments over quality of instruction
- Offering fragmented strategies rather than integrated systemic strategies

International evidence strongly supports Fullan's conclusions. A McKinsey study (Mourshed, Chijioke, & Barber, 2010) finds that in the improving systems in developing countries, there was an equal proportion of accountability and capacity-building activities; in the good-to-great countries, the percentages were 78 percent professional learning and 22 percent accountability.

It is not that accountability is a bad idea. Leaders must ensure that accountability is based on trust rather than distrust. It must include feedback for improved performance. While leaders say that they trust and respect teachers, institutional and individual actions speak louder than words.

Professor Richard Ingersoll (2007) of the University of Pennsylvania studied the sources of professional dissatisfaction for many years. His perspective is not only that of a researcher but also of a teacher in both public and private schools.

He observes:

> One of the big reasons I quit was sort of intangible. But it's very real: It's just a lack of respect. . . . Teachers in schools do not call the shots. They have very little say. They're told what to do; it's a very disempowered line of work. (p. 21)

Personal Trust

Building leadership trust begins with personal trustworthiness. There are three qualities leaders must embrace to establish and build personal trust. Leaders must: (1) do what they say they will do; (2) acknowledge mistakes quickly and openly; and (3) confront conflicts between personal values and the professional environment.

Do What They Say They Will Do

When leaders do what they say they will do, their actions speak volumes. For example, when leaders commit to caring about the lives of individual students, it means they know the names of the people—every staff member and every student—in their building. They not only know frequent visitors to the principal's office but every single student. System leaders make a point to spend time among students and teachers and insist that their colleagues in the central office do the same.

In the years leading up to winning the Broad Prize for the best urban system in the United States, Norfolk, Virginia Superintendent John Simpson and Deputy Thomas Lockamy required that some central office staff members spend at least 70 percent of their time in schools providing direct assistance to teachers and building administrators (C. Lassiter, personal communication, March 24, 2015). Superintendent Stan Sheer, who has led educational systems in Missouri, Colorado, and California, put himself on the substitute teacher roster in order to spend time with students not as the superintendent, but as the only adult in the room and interacting directly with students.

One of the United States' most successful superintendents, with more than forty-five years in that position, is Dennis Peterson. He has guided a succession of systems to unprecedented levels of student achievement. After fifteen years at the helm of the school system in Minnetonka, Minnesota, a partial list of the system's accomplishments include the following:

▸ It raised ACT scores from 23.1 to 26.5, while increasing the number of students taking the ACT and reducing the dropout rate so more low-achieving students also took the test.

▸ Whatever comparison group was used—the top one hundred, two hundred, or four hundred—the students in Minnetonka Public Schools outperformed their peers in private schools. (D. Peterson, personal communication, June 5, 2015)

Peterson contends that trust is personal:

> Make it clear that you can be counted on to follow through, be supportive, to carry out the mission of the district. I trust people until they show me they can't be trusted. For new leaders, trust is such an important commodity that if it's lost, it's very hard to regain. People often won't give you a second chance to reestablish trust. Without trust, it's really hard to get people to follow you. (D. Peterson, personal communication, March 31, 2015)

Acknowledge Mistakes Quickly and Openly

Building personal trust is not about leadership perfection but about admitting and learning from mistakes in a public manner. The gold standard for this sort of public and professional accountability is Richard Elmore's (2011) gem of a book *I Used to Think . . . and Now I Think . . . .* The title suggests a way that every education leader can build trust with colleagues and stakeholders.

When asked to name their mistakes, particularly during job interviews, too many leaders offer pabulum such as "I work too hard" or "Sometimes I care too much." These are not the sort of mistakes that, when admitted, build personal trust. I'm talking about serious errors that, even when embarrassing, provide learning opportunities for the leader and the entire school and system. For example:

"I thought I could do the school budget on my own and, under pressure of missing a deadline, submitted it without having it reviewed by a colleague. I made several calculation errors that caused me embarrassment with the superintendent and almost cost our school several staff positions. Now, even when I think a document is perfect, I always have it reviewed in detail by a colleague."

"I saw a student smoking marijuana right outside the classroom door. Rather than following our protocol for this sort of incident and including our professionally trained security team, I just grabbed the drugs from his hands and started screaming at him. This did nothing to save the student from academic ruin (he dropped out shortly after that). Instead, it ensured that we could not take proper disciplinary action because I failed to follow procedure. Although it's easy to react to situations without thinking through them, I've learned that I need to stop and consider my every action when I'm confronting student misbehavior."

"I was newly divorced and asked a staff member to have coffee with me at a nearby restaurant. I just wanted to talk about school matters outside of school grounds, but he interpreted the invitation as an indication of romantic interest. I was horribly embarrassed, and I'm lucky that I didn't receive a complaint. I've learned that although I can be friendly with my colleagues at work, good morale and discipline dictate that I avoid offsite one-to-one contacts with staff members."

"I was confronted by a reporter after a particularly long and difficult board meeting, and, as superintendent, I felt that I had to respond to the reporter's questions. But the subsequent newscast made it look like I was criticizing members of the board in a public and reckless way. I've learned that while it's important to be respectful of the media, I need to collaborate with the board and my senior leadership team regarding the best way to convey our message. Even when we have inevitable disagreements, I need to be sure that my message is one about policy and not personal criticism."

Some of these mistakes are tragic, and every leader makes mistakes like them. But the difference between inexcusable failures and learning failures is the willingness of the leader to be candid in admitting both the mistake and the lessons learned. Learning from mistakes allows leaders to improve their decision process.

Confront Conflicts Between Personal Values and the Professional Environment

The final way that leaders can build personal trust is by confronting people who conflict with their values and having the courage to address problematic situations. Few people thrive on conflict, and those who do rarely survive as leaders. But many people avoid conflict and regard it as a badge of honor to boast of buy-in from their subordinates. The illusion of a conflict-free environment is a common leadership trap, as it only moves the arguments from a public and potentially constructive forum to parking lots and neighborhood restaurants and bars, where constructive conflict resolution is unlikely.

Worse yet, avoiding conflict creates cynicism, as colleagues listen to leaders' stated values and then observe their tolerance of contemptuous attitudes and destructive actions toward colleagues and students. "She sounds great in public," her colleagues say, "but she never does anything about it when her values are violated." Getting conflict into the open is a challenging but necessary leadership task, and it is the only way that leaders can demonstrate the difference between skeptics and cynics.

Professional Trust

"Authority doesn't come from a title, degree, or position," argues principal and leadership author Thomas Hoerr (2014). "It comes because others believe in us and trust us. They know we care, and they know we listen. This can build up over time, but it can erode quite quickly" (p. 87).

Andy Hargreaves, Alan Boyle, and Alma Harris (2014) studied a variety of organizations. Hargreaves in particular considered the relationship of trust and its impact in diverse organizations, including professional sports teams, businesses, nonprofit organizations, and educational systems. Their conclusions are compelling:

> If you invest your time in building trust, it will pay dividends down the line. It is easier to challenge people who trust you than it is to trust people whom you have only ever been confrontational with previously. . . . Understand that trust takes time to be verified through many interactions; but once you've established it, fleetness of foot and accelerated improvement will come as a result. (pp. 170–171)

This book does not advocate unlimited professional freedom, particularly when freedom means that teachers and administrators can escape observation and objective examination of their impact on students. Professional trust is a two-way street. Both teachers and leaders must begin by giving one another the benefit of the doubt. Leaders should start every day assuming that teachers want to do a good job, that they want to earn respect as professionals, and that they deserve trust. Similarly, teachers should begin every day assuming that principals and other administrators believe in them, trust them, and make decisions based on the best interests of every student in the school.

In their important book *Credibility: How Leaders Gain and Lose It, Why People Demand It*, Kouzes and Posner (2011) make the case that "credibility is the foundation of leadership" (p. xi). Supported by survey data from more than seventy-five thousand leaders and more than one thousand case studies for "my most admired leader," Kouzes and Posner (2011) note:

> The results of our studies over the last three decades have been strikingly consistent. They have remained consistent not only [across] time but also around the world and across care stories of age, gender, ethnicity, functional discipline, organizational level, and the like. . . . What are these crucial attributes? According to our empirical data, the majority of people look for [and] admire leaders who are honest, forward-looking, inspiring, and competent. . . . While the exact rank order might vary from country to country, these same four qualities remain at the top of the list of what people everywhere want from their leaders. (p. 7)

Trust does not require perfection. Instead, it acknowledges our imperfections in a manner that shows authenticity. When mistakes are considered signs of weakness and incompetence, don't expect the absence of mistakes—just the absence of acknowledgment. Neither the leader nor the organization learns from hidden mistakes. Mistakes are opportunities for learning.

Trust and Vulnerability

Expressions of personal and professional trust require the assumption of personal responsibility. Psychiatrist M. Scott Peck began his 1978 global bestseller *The Road Less Traveled* with the sentence, "Life is difficult" (p. 1). While that observation was obvious to most readers, the pages that followed claimed that all of us, but leaders in particular, have two choices when faced with difficult situations. We can assume too much responsibility—a condition that in extreme forms becomes neuroses. "The weather is terrible, and it's all my fault!" The other alternative is even worse, and that is to assume insufficient amounts of responsibility. "I don't know why we can't have the tools we need to be successful; it's somebody in accounting or maybe the superintendent—the board probably is involved in it too. There's nothing I can do."

People with this attitude never see a positive suggestion that they don't run away from. They tend to victimize others and then promptly blame the victim. Nothing is ever their fault, and they are quick to blame subordinates, the economy, and every human and supernatural force except for their own personal responsibility.

Part of earning trust is not only taking personal responsibility for the performance of the team and organization but also being sufficiently vulnerable to take the inevitable criticism. Contrary to the popular myth of the invincible leader, vulnerable people are willing to share their mistakes, frailties, and failures in front of the team.

Ask a spouse, employee, or child who has had his or her trust betrayed by another, and the answer will likely be that broken trust can be repaired, but it takes years, perhaps a lifetime, to accomplish. The good news is that leaders can build trust by (1) doing what they say they will do; (2) acknowledging mistakes quickly and openly; and (3) confronting conflicts between personal values and the professional environment.

In the aptly titled *Leadership BS,* Stanford Professor Jeffrey Pfeffer (2015) suggests that too many discussions about leadership are "like being under the effect of nitrous oxide (laughing gas) . . . by leaving people feeling good while somewhat uninformed about reality. The leadership enterprise helps produce people happily oblivious to many important truths about organizational life in the real world" (p. 195). While we may create an impossible standard for leaders, the truth is that we fail, personally and professionally. Organizations that once felt like a close-knit family grow into unfeeling bureaucracies. The promises made in interviews fade into distant memories as the exigencies of the moment displace long-term values. Marriages that we thought would last forever fail. If the absence of failure is the criterion for successful leadership, then we are left with a choice of either illusions or lies.

When leaders talk about their mistakes, it is an act of courage that sets the tone for the entire organization. Failure, while never fun, happens. What builds and sustains trust is not the absence of failure but the willingness to acknowledge and learn from it.

Just as not acknowledging mistakes is a barrier to effective leadership, so is the well-intended pursuit of too many ideas, too quickly, in too many areas. The remedy for this is focus, the next element of leadership to which we now turn our attention.

CHAPTER 3

FOCUS

The element of focus suggests that successful leaders must make conscious choices not only about what they will do but also about what they will *not* do. These leaders exhibit *calendar integrity*—that is, they use their time in a way that aligns with their values and priorities. This is worth a personal analysis, and you can complete it within just a few minutes. For a full week, keep a detailed record of how you spend your time. Many apps are available that can help you do this quickly and easily and create a pie chart showing your actual time allocation. Compare the pie chart to your top three priorities. The difference is, almost invariably, astounding. I've never heard a superintendent say, "My top priorities are to have meetings about compliance issues, personnel hearings, and board subcommittees," but a quick look at the calendars of many system leaders suggests that these *are* their priorities.

This chapter is about focus and fragmentation. My essential argument is that focused leaders help their colleagues perform better and achieve greater levels of student performance, while fragmented leaders are like moths to the flame of every education fad. The chapter concludes with some practical advice on how leaders can *weed their education gardens* and take precautions against the lure of fragmentation.

The Focus Imperative

While focused leaders are relentless to the point of being boring, fragmented leaders show enthusiasm that gains popularity without impact. Focused leaders require accountability, while fragmented leaders are too busy pushing tomorrow's agenda to recall yesterday's imperatives. Focused leaders pursue sustainable practices, while fragmented leaders chase programs with elusive and illusory claims of proprietary exclusivity. Focused leaders are dull, while fragmented leaders are glamorous. It is no wonder that focused leaders are rare.

In the research involving more than two thousand schools and more than 1.5 million students in a diverse sample of schools in the United States and Canada (Reeves, 2011), only 4 percent of high-poverty schools demonstrated high levels of focus; only 2 percent of schools with large numbers of English learners (ELs) demonstrated high levels of focus; and only 5 percent of schools with large numbers of special education students demonstrated high levels of focus. There is no malice in school leaders who lack focus, only sincere but misguided efforts to solve problems by piling one initiative on top of another, leading to initiative fatigue.

Most schools are composed of an economic and ethnic mix of students. These students might speak dozens of languages other than English, and their test results might appear satisfactory. Into this seductively appealing environment, fragmentation can become the norm. Because everything appears to be working—students are testing well and parents are happy—every new idea from a conference, journal article, or book can displace or distract from focus.

The prevailing theory of change, as illustrated in figure 3.1, suggests that a little more change should lead to test results that are a little bit better. It doesn't matter what the changes are, from where they came, or on what they're based—none of the changes has a chance of success when they are just one more rock on the mountain of change initiatives.

The horizontal axis in figure 3.1 is the degree of change implementation in schools, and the vertical axis is the impact of these changes on student test results. It stands to reason that after a school system has implemented change and invested in professional development–associated technology, then it should see better results.

However, this assumption of linear gains in student achievement is consistently incorrect. In studies of education systems in the United States and Canada, the impact of change on student achievement is distinctly nonlinear (Reeves, 2011). Incremental change does not result in a comparable incremental gain in student achievement. Rather, the greatest gains in achievement happen only at the greatest levels of implementation. Figure 3.2 illustrates this pattern.

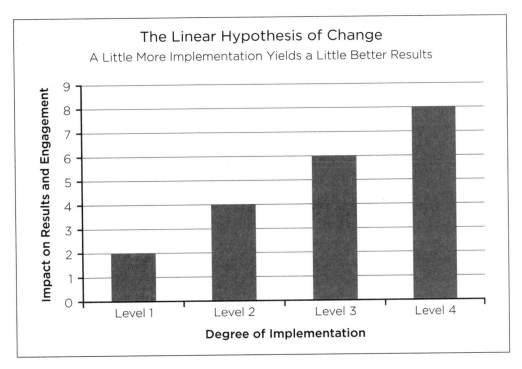

Figure 3.1: The linear hypothesis of change.

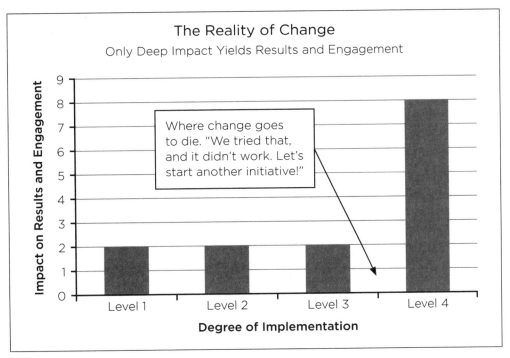

Figure 3.2: The reality of change.

The truth is that *a little bit more* with regard to implementing instructional and leadership initiatives is not associated with improved student achievement. Only at the highest levels of implementation do these initiatives cause significant improvement. The greatest challenge is that too few initiatives ever achieve the highest level of implementation. That is the reason that the space between the third and fourth levels of achievement is, as figure 3.2 (page 33) suggests, where change goes to die.

Rather than reach the highest levels of achievement, school leaders and teachers unanimously claim, "Well, that didn't work, so let's try another initiative." Thus, schools are littered with initiatives that they start but never completely implement. The cause is not a failure of will by teachers and leaders, but rather initiative fatigue, in which too many initiatives compete for attention, denying any of them the time and energy required to attain deep implementation. Getting to the highest levels of implementation of one initiative requires saying *no* to many other initiatives.

Focus on the Best Initiatives

When did you last have the time to focus on an idea, a relationship, or a challenge? I recently watched several rehearsals of the Boston Symphony Orchestra, arguably one of the best ensembles in the world (Gramophone, n.d.). During several three-hour rehearsals conducted by James Levine and Rafael Brubeck de Burgos, I measured the time the musicians actually practiced the music that they would perform within days. The results were stunningly consistent, ranging from 22.8 to 23.4 percent talk-to-practice ratio. I also watched Grammy award–winning conductor Scott Jarrett rehearse the Boston University Marsh Chapel Choir and found almost identical results. Both conductors devoted about 80 percent of their time to practice rather than talk.

Levine, de Burgos, and Jarrett never start at the beginning of a piece of music. Instead, they jump from one section to another, repeating the most difficult passages again and again, with intense focus on the most difficult challenges facing the musicians.

They model what John Hattie (2009) describes as "deliberative practice" (p. 24). What Hattie says about students is also true of adult learners:

> Learning is not always pleasurable and easy; it requires over-learning at certain points, spiraling up and down the knowledge continuum, and building a working relationship with

others in grappling with challenging tasks. This is the power of deliberative practice. It also requires a commitment to seeking further challenges—and herein lies a major link between challenge and feedback, two of the essential ingredients of learning. The greater the challenge, the higher the probability that one seeks and needs feedback, the more important it is that there is a teacher to provide feedback and to ensure that the learner is on the right path to successfully meet the challenges. (p. 24)

This is hardly a new insight, as educators knew of the practice back in 1885 (Simon, 2012). But as is the case with so many research-based practices in education, actual practice lags far behind the research to support it.

The day after watching the Boston Symphony rehearsal, I watched a school administrator conduct a meeting and again clocked the talk-to-practice ratio. It was almost precisely the opposite, with more than 80 percent talk and less than 20 percent practice—that is, in the context of deliberating and learning. Even the practice seemed artificial and forced. It was akin to musicians talking about playing a particularly challenging passage from works by Stravinsky, Shostakovich, and Mozart rather than actually practicing the works that were on the program. Focus is about practice. Fragmentation is about distraction.

In chapter 1, we considered how well-intentioned governing boards pursuing every conceivable purpose rob their organizations of focus. Please take a moment to examine the agenda of your last staff meeting, cabinet meeting, or board meeting. (If there is no agenda, then that speaks for itself.) It is a challenge to enumerate the contents of the agenda items and allotted time and compare them to the officially stated mission and vision of the board. If the two were to be in concert, then the mission of the school system would read something like this:

> Our mission is to ignore evidence and elevate popular opinion. Budgets are far more important than student achievement. Our vision for student achievement is based primarily on the size of the stadium scoreboard, the color of the tile in our newest building, and the comfort of the adults who intend to use the weight room and pool far more frequently than the students. Above all, we intend to elevate the interests of adults above children and maintain the values of employees, parents, and interest groups above those of anyone who can't vote—that is, children younger than eighteen.

Have you ever heard of such a mission statement? I have. But it has never been official. Most damaging are the cases in which implicit missions, inherent in the actions of leaders and policymakers and verified by the observations of students and employees, depart from explicit mission and vision statements. This variation is evidence of hypocrisy that can doom the organization. Although the current leadership may have a clear vision of which initiatives are most important, a different picture emerges at the classroom and school levels.

In one large urban school system that I studied in 2011, teachers and principals identified eighty-eight initiatives compared to the district leadership, which prioritized only six—a ratio of more than 14:1. This was hardly the fault of the current superintendent, whose leadership vision was crystal clear. But his new vision did not displace the initiatives of his predecessors. Rather, from the point of view of teachers and principals, it was one more set of initiatives piled on those previously established and deeply embedded. This system did not engage in the essential discipline of "We will do . . . and therefore, will *not* do . . ." addressed earlier in this chapter.

Contrast the shifting ambiguity of mission and the accompanying large number of unfocused initiatives to the view of Superintendent Dennis Peterson (personal communication, March 31, 2015):

> We only have one focus—student success. We don't focus on adult concerns but what is right for kids. Make sure you don't get diverted into a lot of different strategies. Stick with the right strategies, but discard those that are not working. Too many people try different things but never really know which strategies they're serious about. In our district, administrators and teachers know the central priority. I listen—I don't just state the mission but listen to what they are trying to accomplish. We did an exercise in which we allowed staff members to identify their greatest focus, and they were strongest in unity of purpose. We must live that out every day. It's not just written on a wall. It's how we do things.

After conducting the initiative inventory, school systems must assess the level of implementation of each initiative. Human performance takes place on a continuum. The greatest mistake education systems make is to take a binary approach to implementation—that is, *We did it* or *We didn't do it.* This is the fallacy of delivery—that once the school receives materials and teachers withstand another professional development seminar, then the new initiative has been delivered. But delivery does not equal implementation.

In contrast to the binary fallacy of *We did it* or *We didn't do it*, consider a more nuanced description of implementation in the context of one the most prominent educational reforms of the 21st century—PLCs. PLCs are one of the most widely supported, research-based methods for creating a system of sustainable school improvement (DuFour & Reeves, 2016). The essence of a PLC is teachers and administrators committed to a collaborative process in which they forge clear agreements on what students must know and be able to do, how they will assess students on those key areas, what they will do when students fail to meet those expectations, and how they will provide enrichment opportunities for students who are already excelling at these academic standards (DuFour, DuFour, Eaker, & Many, 2010). The following are some examples of implementation rubrics that schools have applied in the context of their work in PLCs:

▸ **Level 1 (pre-initiating):** People react to conflict with classic flight-or-fight responses. Most staff members withdraw from interactions in order to avoid those they find disagreeable. Others are perpetually at war in acrimonious, unproductive arguments that never seem to get resolved. People seem more interested in winning arguments than in resolving differences. Groups tend to regard each other as adversaries.

▸ **Level 2 (initiating):** School and district leaders take steps to resolve conflict as quickly as possible. People view addressing conflict as an administrative responsibility. The primary objective of administrators in addressing disputes is to restore the peace.

▸ **Level 3 (developing):** Staff members have created norms or protocols to help them identify and address the underlying issues causing conflict. Members receive encouragement to explore their positions and the fundamental assumptions that have led them to their positions. They attempt to use a few key guiding principles to assist them in coming to closure.

▸ **Level 4 (sustaining):** Staff members view conflict as a source of creative energy and an opportunity for building shared knowledge. They create specific strategies for exploring one another's thinking, and they make a conscious effort to understand as well as to be understood.

They seek ways to test competing assumptions through action research and are willing to rethink their position when research, data, and information contradict their suppositions. Because they have found common ground on their purpose and priorities, they are able to approach disagreements with high levels of trust and an assumption of good intentions.

There is striking evidence of the impact of PLCs on student achievement (Reeves, 2015a), but this relationship only occurs when schools implement PLCs with fidelity and with the expectation that the shift will be long term. Specifically, in reviewing almost two hundred schools with more than 750,000 students, I found that schools that had followed the PLC model for seven years or longer had significantly greater gains than those that had implemented PLCs for only two or three years.

Finally, leaders must compare each initiative's level of implementation to gains in student achievement. This allows leaders to separate the initiatives into four quadrants, as illustrated in figure 3.3. The lower-left quadrant includes initiatives with low impact and low implementation levels. Its name, Weed, suggests that these initiatives are easy to weed out. After all, they have no impact and nobody is using them.

Evaluate, the lower-right quadrant, includes popular initiatives that are being implemented but with little impact on achievement. These are the shiny objects that capture the attention of organizational leaders. This category includes technology initiatives that are devoid of instructional content and motivational rallies that provide a temporary spark of emotional engagement. Initiatives in this quadrant require clear-eyed evaluation.

Initiatives in the upper-left quadrant, Lead, are the most challenging. They have a high impact on student learning but are unpopular and seldom implemented. Formative assessment is one important example. Evidence suggests the strategy is strongly associated with improved student achievement (Hattie, 2012). But when teachers and parents rebel against over-testing, sound assessment practices like formative assessment face a formidable challenge. The Lead quadrant got its name because leaders must discern between those initiatives that deserve implementation, even when unpopular, and those that might be popular and deserve to be eliminated.

The upper-right quadrant, Invest, with high impact and high implementation, requires investment from leaders. Why invest in what is already working? A cardinal principle of leadership is that it is faster and more effective to maximize strengths than to perseverate about weaknesses (Mann & Harter, 2016).

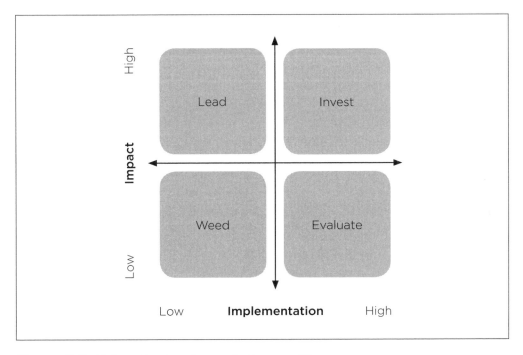

Figure 3.3: Using the implementation audit.

Weed

Each quadrant suggests a different leadership action. The Weed quadrant includes those programs with low levels of implementation and little impact on student achievement. There is no malice here—just the failure to successfully implement programs that might have been well-intentioned a decade ago, but in the course of the intervening years, no longer meet the needs of a school system. Although it might seem obvious that these programs must be weeded out, my experience has taught me that *every turkey has a champion*. In other words, every program will have an advocate, even if the program lacks demonstrable impact—a turkey. It can be difficult to admit that a program has outlived its usefulness.

Sometimes the persistence of bad instructional programs is due to a relationship between the vendor and the purchasing decision maker. Sometimes it is due to true believers who elevate their personal feelings about a program over the evidence. This is particularly true in computerized grading practices, which have the veneer of 21st century learning because they use complex platforms. But the use of 14th century assessments (multiple-choice tests pioneered in the Ming Dynasty) and medieval grading practices (grading as punishment in attempt to motivate) placed on the most sophisticated computer do not render these outdated and ineffective practices into 21st century skills.

Evaluate

The lower-right quadrant, Evaluate, includes deeply implemented programs with questionable evidence of impact on student achievement. These programs require more careful evaluation. For example, it is entirely possible that the culprit for a lack of association between student achievement and the depth of implementation of these programs is the wrong testing instrument. One example might be a school that implements a dual-language immersion program to teach mathematics but only tests mathematics proficiency in English. Another example is using a standardized test designed to assess a wide spectrum of cognitive ability and curriculum knowledge for students whose courses have not prepared them for its content.

Because in some instances state officials require these tests, the best that schools can do is to place the scores into context. "There are many ways in which a school can be accountable for performance," the superintendent might explain to the community, "and state-required tests is only one of them. We are not opposed to accountability, but we insist on putting each accountability measure into its proper context by sharing other data from our schools that better reflect evidence of achievement in all the areas where our students excel."

Such an evaluation also identifies programs that are simply not succeeding despite high levels of implementation. As Grant Wiggins (2015) suggests, even widely accepted models in core subjects like reading require adjustment and adaptation as we learn more about the research relating teacher practice to student achievement. With these adjustments, it's possible to move programs from the Evaluate quadrant into the Invest quadrant (see page 43).

Lead

Lead includes initiatives that have high impact but low implementation. A common example is nonfiction writing, a strategy with a substantial research base associating it with improved student achievement (MacArthur, Graham, & Fitzgerald, 2008). John Hill, assistant superintendent for instruction for Elkhart Community Schools in Elkhart, Indiana, reports that the use of nonfiction writing in every grade and every subject correlates with his district's recognition as the most improved urban district in Indiana.

Originally, the district feared that such an emphasis on writing would detract from essential learning in other subjects. In fact, Hill noted, nonfiction writing was the leverage point that helped students in all subjects. Moreover, with higher success rates in academic subjects, students also enjoyed increased participation in extracurricular activities. In an interview, Hill explained:

> The ten-year progression of Elkhart Community Schools has included a more than 24 percent increase in high school graduation rates, and a steady increase in pass rates of Indiana high-stakes tests every year by almost every identifiable group of our 13,000 students in grades K–12. Many full grade levels of students are now displaying more than 90 percent pass rates on ISTEP+ statewide tests. During the same span of years, participation in band, orchestra, choir, high-ability classes, visual arts, advanced placement, and dual-credit classes also increased, countering a national trend of decreased enrollments in the era of high-stakes testing. (J. Hill, personal communication, June 10, 2015)

Although the Common Core State Standards place a particular emphasis on nonfiction writing, this instructional initiative had value well before the advent of the Common Core. Nevertheless, many teachers find it too time consuming, and those outside of English language arts classes contend that they are not writing teachers. The answer is not another new initiative for writing, but rather leadership for deeper implementation of the writing initiatives that schools already have.

Another example from the Lead quadrant is the establishment of effective grading practices. As Tom Guskey (2014) has demonstrated, the implementation of effective grading practices, such as eliminating the zero on a one hundred–point scale, stopping the use of the average, using grades as a reflection of student learning, and avoiding using grades to enforce compliance and behavior, can have enormous positive benefits. These benefits include not only higher student achievement but also lower dropouts and improved discipline.

There is no question that this is a high-impact initiative. Nevertheless, implementation of grading reform remains very low in the United States and around the world. The situation is reminiscent of the times in which a substantial number of teachers and administrators genuinely believed that corporal punishment—slaps, switches, or boards used to hit students—improved their behavior. Most schools did away with the practice because overwhelming research proved that corporal punishment is counterproductive (Center for Parenting Education, n.d.).

The Lead quadrant is the single greatest challenge for education leaders. They have high-impact initiatives all around them, but they do not implement them. They wait for the illusion of buy-in, for the staff to coalesce around a vision and gain understanding through another interminable professional development speech, and for parents and school board members to agree. It's sometimes as if leaders, whose people are desperate for life-sustaining fresh water, stood before a cool spring but couldn't decide to take the spring water back to their people because they didn't know if the people would agree that it was a good idea.

Education achievement—particularly reducing failures and dropouts—is a public health and safety issue, as the Alliance for Excellent Education (n.d.a) has documented in detail. When leaders confront the Lead quadrant, they have the greatest opportunity to make an immediate impact on student learning. They have the tools, the evidence, and probably at least a few islands of excellence where these high-impact strategies have been working.

Leaders now face two challenges. The first is fear of conflict. The opposition to effective grading practices can be bitter and emotional. The second is the illusion of action, often fueled by participation in a sort of echo chamber where leaders hear their words reflected back in an encouraging tone and their laments about lack of implementation met with soothing understanding. Twitter chats, conferences, and casual conversations can all be part of the echo chamber, where leaders hear only affirmation and from people with whom they agree.

Leaders' determination to act is essential; they must be secure in the knowledge that they are pursuing the best interests of students, even when those actions are unpopular. It is the same determination required of the education leaders who stopped corporal punishment, promoted integration, and dismantled ineffective teaching methods and replaced them with better ones. All of these reforms occurred not because leaders were popular but because they were effective.

Invest

Although it might seem obvious that leaders should preserve the Invest quadrant—high implementation of high-impact instructional practices—the greater challenge is to expand these practices. Left alone, Invest quadrant practices remain islands of excellence in most education systems.

The use of technology in the classroom illustrates this point. Consider the growing ubiquity of SMART Boards (or whiteboards), electronic surfaces on which teachers and students display material and engage in interactive learning processes. Robert Marzano conducted a study—funded by Promethean, a manufacturer of electronic display boards—of more than two hundred classrooms (Manzo, 2010). Both advocates and critics of SMART Boards can find evidence in the study they might want to cherry-pick. According to Kathleen Kennedy Manzo's *Education Week* summary of the report:

> The Promethean boards [electronic boards that projected content from a computer and included opportunities for student interaction] were most effective when they gave students multiple opportunities to use the boards and the interactive features. Nearly one-fourth of the teachers, though, were more effective without [the electronic boards].
>
> That finding highlights one of Marzano's key conclusions from the study. The teachers who were most effective using the whiteboards displayed many of the characteristics of good teaching in general: They paced the lesson appropriately and built on what students already knew; they used multiple media, such as text, pictures, and graphics, for delivering information; they gave students opportunities to participate; and they focused mainly on the content, not the technology.
>
> "These are things good teachers would do without technology," Marzano says. "Technically, you don't need to use the technology, but it's just so hard to do all these things without it."

These findings are consistent with other reports of technology implementation that I reviewed. Although the hardware and software might have potential, a significant number of teachers either do not use them at all or do not use them to achieve their instructional potential. The investment, therefore, is not necessarily in new hardware, but rather in the time it takes for teachers to collaborate in small groups. This allows teachers to see not just the theoretical potential of a piece of technology but also its actual application in their subject areas.

Assess Initiative Implementation

I have found the most effective way of assessing the implementation of education initiatives is to use a three- or four-level rubric, similar to those teachers use in classrooms to assess student performance. The purpose is not merely to provide a final score but also to be a roadmap for improvement to the next level of learning. For example, one major study used a three-level rubric to help leaders establish precise and comprehensive goals for school improvement (Reeves, 2011).

Sometimes the act of listing initiatives and writing an implementation rubric for each one can illustrate just how fragmented a system really has become. It is difficult to focus on the most effective initiatives if you cannot clearly identify the totality of the initiatives vying for attention or how to implement them. At this point, vendors and advocates have succumbed to the binary fallacy of *We did it* or *We didn't do it*, rather than the nuance that instructional practices and programs are implemented at varying degrees. The three-level rubric (Reeves, 2011) illustrates this point, and such an implementation continuum can help leaders guide colleagues on a journey toward success.

The following are guidelines used for more than two thousand schools. By applying the same leadership rubric at the system level (or even the state and provincial levels), senior leaders can systematically identify the relationship between initiative implementation and student results. With regard to leadership goal setting, I used the following three levels: exemplary, proficient, and needs improvement. A partial set of performance descriptions for specific (the first element of SMART) goal setting includes the following (Reeves, 2011):

▸ **Exemplary:** All goals and supporting targets specify targeted student groups, grade level, and standard or content area, with subskills delineated in that content area. Leaders specify assessments to address subgroup needs.

▸ **Proficient:** More than one goal and supporting target specify targeted student groups, grade level, and standard or content area, with subskills delineated in that content area. Leaders specify assessments to address subgroup needs.

> ▶ **Needs improvement:** Most goals and supporting targets describe general rather than specific targeted student groups, grade level, and standard or content area, with subskills delineated in that content area.

Another particularly powerful example deals with the measurability of goals. In reviewing thousands of school plans, this area can create considerable tension among the central office, principals, and teachers. In resisting quantifiable goals, the quote, often misattributed to Albert Einstein and stated with more enthusiasm than accuracy, is sometimes the first volley in the argument, "Not everything that counts can be counted, and not everything that can be counted counts" (Cameron, 1963, p. 13).

This quote, which is actually from the lesser-known William Bruce Cameron, makes sense. Teachers see everyday student and adult behavior that seems immune to quantification. The same might be true of any profession that is part art and part science. We can count the number of times teachers provide feedback to students, and we can certainly count students' test scores, just as we can count the number of patients who die on the operating table and the number of times physicians wash their hands before touching their patients. But what about those things we can't count?

Harvard Medical School Professor and Surgeon Atul Gawande (2007) explains that improvement in any professional practice requires ingenuity and creativity, "but these qualities demand more than anything a willingness to recognize failure, to not paper over the cracks, and to change. It arises from deliberate, even obsessive, reflection on failure and a constant searching for new solutions" (p. 9).

To those who resist the nature of quantitative assessment of leadership, consider the following list of easily quantifiable standards, each of which provides leaders and teachers with the opportunity to monitor improvement throughout the year (Reeves, 2009b):

- Percentage of faculty meeting discussions and action items related to student achievement
- Percentage of professional development activities directly related to classroom practice supporting student achievement
- Percentage of parents who agree or strongly agree with the statement, "I feel welcome to visit my child's classroom at any time"

- Frequency of recognition of teacher best practices

- Percentage of A-level tasks on the leader's daily, prioritized task list directly related to improved student achievement

- Percentage of faculty members with student achievement practices in assessment, curriculum, and instruction at the *distinguished* (or other top-level descriptor) level, according to a collaboratively scored rubric of professional practices

- Percentage of available time by certified staff members devoted to student contact

- Percentage of students with identified academic deficiency who are rescheduled for additional assistance within thirty days of the identified need

- Percentage of leader-initiated parent contacts related to academic achievement (p. 191)

Another common source of resistance to quantification is the number of factors in student performance over which teachers and schools have no control. It is certainly true that teachers cannot control everything that their students experience. Hattie (2009) estimates that socioeconomic status has an effect size of about 0.5, far greater than many instructional programs, but not nearly as great as others, including effective feedback for student learning. Thus, although teachers cannot influence students' socioeconomic status, they certainly can influence many other factors with even greater impact than socioeconomic status.

Gawande (2007) explains that the same is true in medicine. Consider his observations of a hospital in India:

> Using just textbooks and advice from one another, the surgeons at this ordinary district hospital in India had developed an astonishing range of expertise.
>
> What explains this? There was much the surgeons had no control over: the overwhelming flow of patients, the poverty, the lack of supplies. But where they had control—their skills, for example—these doctors sought betterment. They understood themselves to be part of a larger world of medical knowledge and accomplishment. Moreover, they believed that they could measure up in it. . . . They came to feel they could do anything they set their minds to. Indeed, they believed not only that they were part of the larger world but also that they could contribute to it. (p. 244)

An essential element of leadership and teaching is rigorous self-examination and a commitment to improvement. If leaders insist on quantification in the classroom, then they must lead by example. Leaders can show that they walk the talk with calendar integrity—that is, how they spend their time reflects their values. If their values include improved instruction and achievement, then they can determine the amount of their time they spend in classrooms and also the frequency with which they give meaningful feedback to teachers.

Most important, they can determine the frequency with which teachers use that feedback for improvement. Leaders can count the minutes in staff meetings or other gatherings used to provide information compared to the minutes used for genuine collaboration and reflection. Boards and superintendents' cabinets can do the same, rigorously accounting for how they spend their time and comparing those measurements to their expressed values, mission, and vision.

Weed Your Education Garden

As every gardener knows, spring planting carries with it both joys and burdens. Into a fresh patch of rich soil, gardeners can plant seeds, and within weeks, watch the product of their work grow into young flowers and vegetables. However, these are not the only occupants of the garden. Depending on your part of the world, various uninvited guests soon occupy the garden. In some places, noxious grasses rob nutrients and moisture from the plants. In other places, a thistle wraps itself around the plants and strangles the life out of them. Weeds do not need analyses, lectures, or strategic plans. They need to be pulled out by the roots and discarded. Gardeners know that weeds return and, therefore, weeding the garden is not a single act but the regular occupation of a diligent gardener who someday will enjoy an abundant harvest of beautiful flowers and nutritious vegetables.

When was the last time you weeded your education garden? This means clearing the classrooms of irrelevant materials, the agendas of collaborative meetings, and leadership forums of obsolete and unhelpful items. In professional development meetings, I have often challenged the group to think of just one practice, program, or initiative that they could give up. The most common answer is, "We can't; they are all mandated." In these circumstances, I turn directly to the principal or superintendent and ask, "Are all of these practices and programs really mandated?" Uniformly, the answer is a variation of "Some are and some aren't." This opens the door to a conversation about what the system can eliminate. Focus is not possible without thoughtful identification and elimination of the weeds in your education garden.

One good place leaders can start weeding the garden is school and district plans. These documents are almost always designed to demonstrate compliance—sometimes with state or other governing body requirements, sometimes to conform to grant requirements, and sometimes out of tradition. Questions I always ask principals and superintendents are, "How do you use your plan to make decisions? How does your plan help you agree or disagree with new proposals?" Leaders can use these two questions as a filter to drastically reduce many exhausting school and district plans.

Leaders also should help classroom teachers weed their education gardens. A good place to start weeding the education garden is to compare teacher evaluation systems with classroom practices. If, for example, the evaluator is going to look for evidence of lesson plans, standards-based instruction, and effective feedback on learning goals, then these are probably non-negotiable and should stay in place. But that leaves many other initiatives, often involving teacher presentations, that leaders can cut partially or wholly from the classroom.

Compare, for example, the imperative of common formative assessments—the bedrock of systematically measuring achievement against standards—with the vast majority of homework teachers assign. The burden of time for both students and teachers is nearly out of control, yet there is little evidence that most homework is any more than an exercise in compliance. "Good" homework completion, for example, might be a student answering thirty questions correctly.

Imagine if a basketball player practiced a shot, and he or she made that shot thirty consecutive times. At some point, wouldn't a good coach suggest a different shot and some interleaved practice? Would a music teacher insist that a student play the same C-major scale thirty times, or would he or she suggest alternatives? Conversely, if these students were struggling with a basketball shot or a C-major scale, would the teacher require that they make the same mistake thirty times in a row before intervening to help them perform better?

One reason teachers find it difficult to focus is the sheer magnitude of tasks that they and their students encounter every day. They assign homework because parents expect it, teachers believe in it, and it is part of the school culture. But when teachers and students are mired in homework, they sometimes are unable to focus on the most essential elements of teaching and learning.

I encourage education leaders to take a random sample of just one homework assignment from each school, each grade level, and each department. Leaders can easily do this during classroom walkthroughs or other observations. Just look at the homework teachers assign for the day, usually written on the board. If it calls for exercises from the book, make a copy; if it's a worksheet, ask for an extra one. Then, after removing the teacher's name from the assignments, ask a group of teachers and administrators to evaluate each assignment, considering the following five hallmarks of good homework (Vatterott, 2010):

1. **Purpose:** The purpose of homework is practice. With this in mind, Cathy Vatterott suggests several alternatives to the dull repetition of many homework assignments.

2. **Efficiency:** Projects that require nonacademic skills (such as cutting, gluing, or drawing) are often inefficient. Vatterott counsels that "instead of making a diorama of life during the Reconstruction after the United States Civil War, students could write a diary entry as though they were living in the time, discussing daily life, race relations, and laws that affected them" (p. 11).

3. **Ownership:** The key here is choice. This principle does not mean students get free rein; instead, teachers must consider a menu of options and express different ways to approach a learning goal, from multiplication tables to reading requirements.

4. **Competence:** Vatterott states emphatically that we must abandon a one-size-fits-all approach. Homework that students cannot do without help is *not* good homework; students are discouraged when they are unable to complete homework on their own (Darling-Hammond & Ifill-Lynch, 2006; Stiggins, 2007). To ensure homework is doable, teachers must differentiate assignments so they are at the appropriate level of difficulty for individual students (Tomlinson, 2008).

   A simple means of differentiating is to make homework *time based* instead of *task based*. Instead of assigning all students twenty questions to answer, assign all students to complete what they can in a specified amount of time, for example, "Answer as many questions as you can in thirty minutes; work longer if you like."

5. **Aesthetic appeal:** "Five-page worksheets or endless lists of definitions or math problems look boring and tedious. . . . Wise teachers have

learned that students at all levels are more motivated to complete assignments that are visually uncluttered. Less information on the page, plenty of room to write answers, and the use of graphics or clip arts make tasks look inviting and interesting" (Vatterott, p. 14).

To Vatterott's list of hallmarks, I would add that some of the practice should be independent practice, and some should be guided practice. The guided practice might include the teacher or a fellow student.

We know that one of the most powerful influences on student learning is feedback, but in order for feedback to be effective, it must be timely and specific. The temporal distance between sitting at the kitchen table and completing, or failing to complete, a homework assignment one evening or perhaps several days afterward is an eternity to students. It's far better that teachers create time during class for homework so students who require a greater challenge can receive it immediately, and students who struggle can receive support immediately. As my principal Mr. Robinson wisely said, "The word *homework* may or may not have anything to do with the word *home* (R. Robinson, personal communication, February 1, 1995).

Consider how you might apply these hallmarks of effective homework to leadership tasks. One of the most consistent complaints I hear from leaders is the amount of time they spend away from their primary mission of instructional leadership. Deanna Housefeld, former assistant to the superintendent in Milwaukee Public Schools in the 1990s, helped alleviate this problem when she noticed that principals were receiving multiple demands—often for the same information—from different central office departments. Housefeld created the One Plan, in which all information requests went to her. One Plan pledged to each principal that he or she would receive information requests only one time.

When I examine school plans over the course of time, I notice that many of them are exactly the same from one year to another and that a substantial amount of the content is responsive not to school needs but to the format needs of a higher authority. One of the most important ways to divert leadership time from bureaucratic imperatives to instructional goals is to systematize the manner in which leaders create school plans.

The ultimate goal should be the "plan on a page," expressing the singular goal of student improvement and, within a very few lines, the goals, strategies, and actions the school will undertake to achieve those goals. In most education systems, this does not conform to the format requirements of external authorities, but it certainly could be an effective cover page—the primary area of focus for principals and teachers to actually implement the plans that relate the most to improvements in student achievement.

Sustain Focus

Although I will address the issue of sustainability more fully in chapter 7, the issue of sustaining focus deserves special attention. Focus—for leaders, education systems, schools, and classrooms—is the essence of closing the gap between what we *know* and what we *do*. Mike Schmoker (2011) reduces the essentials of focus to four areas: (1) curriculum, (2) lessons, (3) meaningful reading and writing, and (4) implementation, including monitoring of implementation. Specifically, he claims:

> We know what a sound, coherent curriculum is. Let's build one in every course we teach, with common assessments, and then actually monitor to ensure that it's being taught.
>
> We know—now more than ever—that structurally sound lessons will literally multiply the number of students who will be ready for college, careers, and citizenship.
>
> We know that students desperately need to do lots of meaningful reading and writing . . . and that this does not necessitate inordinate amounts of paper grading. Let's stop making excuses for not doing it.
>
> We know that the implementation of all of the above relies on our commitment to monitor that implementation and encourage teachers to work in teams to help each other to refine and improve on their design and execution. If they do, each of the above will improve dramatically and inexorably. It's that simple. (p. 217)

Avoid the Lure of Fragmentation

Leadership focus is particularly important in schools that face the greatest challenges. Therefore, you might think that these schools would display the greatest degree of leadership focus. But in the many school plans that I studied (Reeves, 2011), only 4 percent of high-poverty schools scored the highest rating on focus, while 30 percent scored at the lowest level. Schools with high proportions of students who speak a second language rarely showed high levels of focus, with only 2 percent of schools earning the highest rating.

Why does this happen? Let's call it the *grant illusion*—the misconception that, because resources are scarce in high-poverty schools, they should chase and accept whatever grant money they can find. Consider the case of data analysis, something every school needs. Who wouldn't want to make better leadership and teaching decisions based on data?

Delaware was an early winner of the federally funded Race to the Top grants. Soon after the grant was awarded in 2010, I sat in a room full of professional service providers all explaining how they were going to use grant funds to help Delaware schools. No fewer than seven of them said they would go to each school and help teachers and administrators gather and use their data. Despite the system's prodigious technology investment, most data analysis vendors required teachers to engage in laborious data entry processes, using the vendor's three-ring binders to accumulate data. No sooner had one vendor finished than another came in, providing many of the same services.

The same cycle—high financial need and pursuit of grant funds, followed by inundation with duplicative requirements—plays out in many jurisdictions. The school officials and presumably the vendors have good intentions. But the proliferation of the same services took valuable time from teachers already stretched to the breaking point. However good an idea may be, these overlapping and duplicative efforts contribute little to improved teaching and learning.

Only a few leaders have said, "We're not going to seek or accept funds that divert us from our primary mission to improve teaching and learning. We have a solid plan to do that, and we have no time or energy to add multiple initiatives on top of what we already have, even if accepting those burdens would (at least on the surface) provide us with more money."

Time is at a premium, especially for educators. It takes courage to stop the fragmentation, weed the garden, and reallocate time to instructional and leadership practices that have the greatest potential impact. Most staff meetings are where systems could recover hundreds of hours of professional time. Instead, that time could be devoted to collaborative scoring, developing common formative assessments, and sharing effective instructional strategies. Consider the variance in schools in the same system—the same per-pupil funding, teacher assignment policies, and union contracts, as well as similar student demographics. Some juggle dozens of initiatives, while others focus on fewer than half a dozen.

When you build a foundation of purpose and trust, colleagues will rely on you to make the difficult judgment calls that lead to focus. When a school is properly focused, it discovers the leverage points that yield the greatest impact on student learning. The next chapter explains how to find and apply the principles of leverage.

CHAPTER 4

LEVERAGE

In the 2nd century before the Common Era, Greek mathematician Archimedes said, "Give me a place to stand and with a lever I will move the whole world" (The Lever, n.d.). Though physicists have engaged in some entertaining debates about how long that lever would have to be, they agree that Archimedes was right—leverage is powerful. Finding leverage in education systems, however, can be challenging. Some leadership and instructional strategies with the greatest leverage—the greatest result for the least investment of time, energy, and resources—are not very popular. Moreover, when lots of little levers compete for a leader's attention, the few big levers are lost. The central question you must address as a leader is not just what activities have potential leverage over education results but what few activities have the *greatest* leverage.

The Wrong Question

What Works Clearinghouse (http://ies.ed.gov/ncee/wwc) is a source of evidence-based interventions in schools from the U.S. Department of Education Institute of Education Sciences. The institute rigorously screens various programs and initiatives and more than ten thousand studies in order to narrow the hundreds of programs available. It helps schools focus on what is most effective. Despite these good intentions, however, the institute still provides twenty-two interventions for third-grade reading alone and seven for dropout prevention. It's nice to have choices, but making *good* choices is essential. Schools flooded with multitudes of strategies and initiatives aimed at the same objective find it difficult to execute all of them well.

While U.S. government efforts to provide leaders research-based alternatives may help schools sort out competing claims, virtually every vendor can produce evidence that its offerings are research based and that its programs work—that is, there is some evidence that the programs are associated with improved student achievement. If schools were to accept the What Works standard for implementing educational initiatives, they would still be drowning in more initiatives than they could possibly implement.

This is why assessing the *degree* of implementation for each initiative is so important. Instructional interventions that pass the What Works standard with flying colors only are effective if implemented deeply. For example, research shows that when students write competently, they improve their performance in other areas, including reading, science, and social studies (Reeves, 2002a).

However, merely purchasing a writing curriculum or sending teachers to a workshop is insufficient. Two teachers with the same training, same time, and same curricular resources might practice very different levels of implementation. Let's assume both teachers administer the same writing prompts and use the same scoring rubric. Even then, one might use the scoring rubric as a teacher-directed evaluation device at the end of the assignment. But the other teacher, implementing more deeply, might help students apply that scoring rubric to their own writing and that of their peers. This teacher will have evidence of students editing, revising, and improving their writing, and demonstrate the application of writing skills in many different parts of the curriculum. Both teachers implemented the writing curriculum, but one clearly implemented at a much deeper level. Given the limits of time, professional energy, and student attention, it's folly to simultaneously implement multiple initiatives. Leadership should not ask, "What works?" but rather, "What works best for the students in our school?"

The Right Question

Gawande (2007) found that the hallmark of hospital improvement includes not only measurements of results but also regular reflection on those results and how they should influence professional practices in the future. Similarly, Hattie

(2012) suggests that the calculation of effect size is not merely the province of researchers; classroom teachers can and should know their impact on student results. Specifically, they can measure student achievement before and after a specific teaching intervention and compare the results.

The easiest way to do this is a spreadsheet with three columns: student name in the first column, student score on the first test in the second column, and student score on the second test in the third column. Electronic spreadsheet programs can automatically calculate the effect size for the entire class. With Excel, for example, highlight the entire first and second columns, and then use the Excel Effect Size command. See the two-minute Vimeo explanation at https://vimeo .com/57012651 to find a guided tour of how to do this for your school.

For people who prefer to do the mathematics by hand, instructions are available in *Visible Learning for Teachers* (Hattie, 2012). This spreadsheet is a good indicator of student learning compared to, for example, a before-and-after bar chart, because it allows the teacher and school leaders to compare the effect sizes of different interventions and make midcourse corrections accordingly. Most important, it allows educators to identify persistently low effect sizes and remove ineffective programs and practices in order to make way for those with the greatest promise for influencing student results. This supports the question leaders ask about initiatives, "What works best for the students in our school?"

How to Measure Leverage

The key to measuring leadership leverage is not proving correlation between one or another initiative and gains in student achievement. Rather, leaders must test prevailing hypotheses and support or disprove them with data, or conclude that the data are inconclusive. For example, one hypothesis is that students can only demonstrate knowledge on material that they have been taught. As logical as that may sound, sometimes it is not true. A very simple preassessment reveals knowledge before a lesson is taught, giving the teacher valuable insights and saving instructional time. Teachers also save time when they don't present information requiring prior knowledge that students lack. Another common hypothesis is that teachers do not have time to teach and assess writing across the curriculum. The fallacy is that they do not have time to cover their content as well as writing. As you will see, that too is a testable hypothesis.

Nonfiction Writing

For example, think about how you might interpret the chart in figure 4.1. The line on the graph represents the relationship between the frequency of student writing (the horizontal axis) and student achievement results in reading, writing, and mathematics (the vertical axis). Think for a moment about how the graph might look if the data supported various hypotheses. One hypothesis might be: If we spend more time on student writing, then we won't have time for reading and mathematics instruction, and scores in those two vital subjects will go down. If evidence supports that hypothesis, the line would go from the upper-left corner down to the lower-right corner. As the frequency of writing assessment increases, scores in reading and mathematics would go down.

I investigated this assumption with several thousand students (Reeves, 2002a). The simplified results of my investigation, shown in figure 4.1, reveal that the more nonfiction writing assessment students engaged in, the higher their scores in reading, writing, and mathematics. It's not a perfect relationship. Sometimes students spent a lot of time on writing and did badly in the other subjects, and sometimes they did well in those subjects without spending a lot of time on writing. But for the most part, more writing is strongly associated with better performance in other subjects.

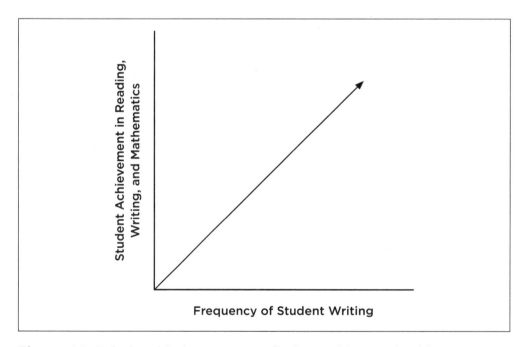

Figure 4.1: Relationship between nonfiction writing and achievement.

Whenever you observe two such strongly related variables, it's very tempting to exclaim, "Eureka! It's clear that as students write more, student achievement increases!" That's possible, particularly if, over time, one were to observe the same results in a variety of student settings, and if there were a control group in which some randomly selected students don't receive the opportunity for writing and others do. That sort of research, as I observed in "Galileo's Dilemma: The Illusion of Scientific Certainty in Educational Research" (Reeves, 2002b), requires an ethical breach that no researcher should consider. How would you feel if your children were assigned to the control group and thus denied the opportunity for potentially effective instructional interventions? I conclude that real science involves ambiguity, experimentation, and error. However distasteful that trio may be, it is far superior to political agendas, uninformed prejudice, and breathless enthusiasm for the flavor of the month.

How can we apply these principles to an accurate interpretation of the data shown in figure 4.1? First, when we only consider two variables, we eliminate a lot of other elements that we might associate with student achievement. Perhaps, for example, students with high socioeconomic status not only write more but also have higher student achievement—so the real variable is not writing but student wealth. Perhaps students who write more are in school systems that value writing and where teachers focus more on student success—so the real variable is not writing but teacher quality. You get the idea—life is multivariate. There is rarely one cause for one effect.

Instead, how can we interpret the data in figure 4.1 in an accurate and modest way? Rather than seek the futile path of proving cause and effect, let's consider what we can disprove. For example, we can disprove the statement, "If we spend more time on writing, I won't have time to cover all of the standards, and therefore, student achievement will decline." Figure 4.1 clearly disproves this hypothesis. While we can't say that writing is the cause of improved student achievement, we can certainly refute the hypothesis that devoting time to writing leads to decreased student achievement.

Professional Learning Communities (PLCs)

We can make a similar observation about PLCs. As figures 4.2–4.4 (pages 60–61) demonstrate, there is certainly a strong relationship between the implementation duration of PLCs and improvements in student achievement.

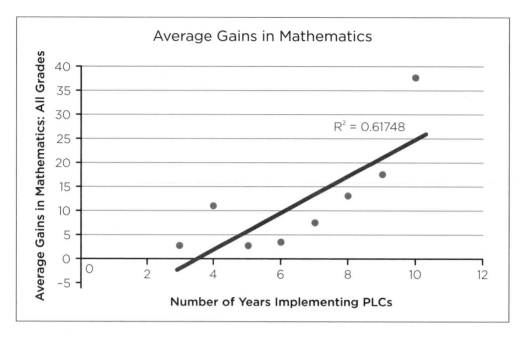

Source: Adapted from Reeves, 2015b.

Figure 4.2: PLCs and achievement in mathematics.

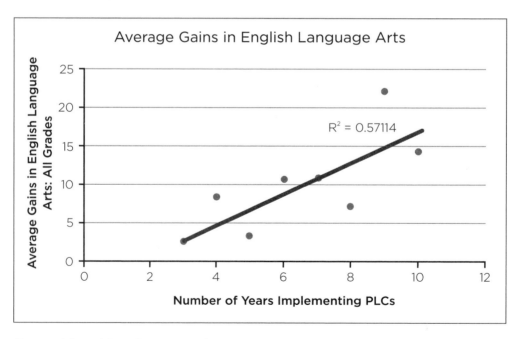

Source: Adapted from Reeves, 2015b.

Figure 4.3: PLCs and achievement in English language arts.

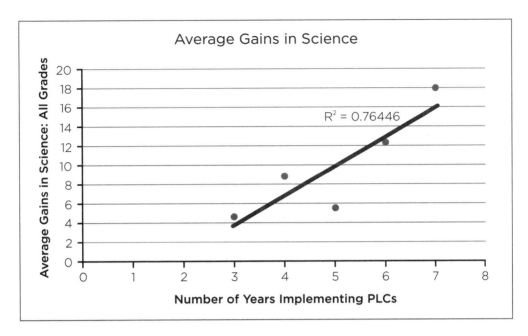

Source: Adapted from Reeves, 2015b.

Figure 4.4: PLCs and achievement in science.

Does this allow us to conclude that PLCs caused improvement in mathematics, English language arts, and science scores? Not yet—even with almost two hundred schools and more than 750,000 students in the sample. Leaders should be modest in their research claims, particularly when they hear someone say, "Research shows that . . . ." The most accurate inference to draw from these charts is that when someone claims, "We don't have time for PLCs, because if we devoted time to them, our student achievement would decline," the contention is clearly wrong.

There may be many reasons why these charts show a positive relationship between PLCs and student achievement, and the implementation of PLCs is surely not the only cause of these achievement gains. But we can say with a high degree of confidence that the time devoted to PLCs does not *diminish* achievement. Once we lower the risk of a proposed instructional strategy, then it is up to teachers and leaders to observe the degree to which the strategy actually works for them.

This approach is strikingly different from the claims of most research-based instructional and leadership interventions. Most interventions simply show a *before* and *after* comparison. That's a good start. But the preceding charts show the relationships (in these cases, between student writing and duration of PLCs) for many schools and many students. The standard that education leaders should seek is a preponderance of the evidence, including individual classroom observations, schoolwide case studies, systematic analysis of many schools, meta-analyses of many studies (popularized by Robert Marzano, Tim Waters, and Brian McNulty [2005] in *School Leadership That Works*), and a synthesis of meta-analyses, most notably by Hattie (2009) in *Visible Learning* and subsequent publications.

Effective Feedback

Another teaching strategy strongly associated with improved student achievement is effective feedback that is FAST: fair, accurate, specific, and timely (Reeves, 2016). When students receive feedback that is sufficiently specific and timely, they are able to predict their own grades with a high degree of precision. In fact, of 150 instructional interventions that Hattie (2012) studied, accurate feedback that allowed students to correctly predict their final grade turns out to be the most important. How significant is this singular effect of accurate, specific, and timely feedback? The effect size is almost 1.5. To put that in perspective, the effect size of socioeconomic status is about 0.5. No one is saying that socioeconomic status is irrelevant, but we *can* say that effective feedback—particularly fair, accurate, specific, and timely feedback—matters a great deal more.

Leaders should consider these three high-leverage strategies—nonfiction writing, PLCs, and effective feedback. With deep implementation of each, education leaders can draw their own conclusions about their impact. But without a focus on these ideas, or a very few similar ideas, leaders will fall victim to the fragmentation that remains so prevalent in education systems around the world.

High-Impact Leadership

Australia has been one of America's closest allies and has made disproportionate sacrifices to secure global peace. It also is striving to come to grips with the challenges of its history when Europeans displaced Aboriginal peoples who occupied the country for more than forty thousand years before the settlers colonized and ultimately dominated the country (Western Australia Department of Education and Training, n.d.). Unlike public ceremonies in the United States, where a similar displacement of the original inhabitants took place, Australian public meetings often begin by acknowledging this historical past, a ceremony I have witnessed in each public seminar I have attended in eight visits to that country.

This is a good model for the rest of the world to follow. Before we embrace the latest and greatest, perhaps we should pause for a moment for those who came before us, whether they are the teachers of previous generations or the teachers from the native nations that occupied North America long before Europeans "discovered" it. If we wish to engage in high-impact leadership, we should start not with 21st century demands but rather with the wisdom and traditions of the past.

We also can learn about high-impact leadership from leaders with broad international experience. Jenny Lewis of Australia has too many titles to name, but they include Fellow of the Commonwealth Council for Educational Administration and Management and Fellow of Australian Council for Educational Leaders. When I asked Lewis how she reconciles the demands of 21st century education with actual practice not only in Australia but also around the world, she offered the following observations (J. Lewis, personal communication, March 31, 2015):

First, leaders must build trust through a moral compass. They must be ethical in their practices and in everything that they model and do. Doing so makes it easier for leaders who have to make a hard choice. Followers understand and honor the choices of trustworthy leaders.

Second, leaders must provide a focus. Even with a strategic plan, people do not necessarily know where to focus. Confusion on this point leads to a fragmented approach that causes dilution of strategic plans, and only the leader can lend the clarity that followers need. Unfortunately, poor training for system and school leaders on strategic thinking still leads to reactive plans that don't improve schools.

Third, leaders must focus not only on curriculum and teaching but also on student well-being. Students must be safe and well nourished. This is a responsibility in the developing world as well as in industrialized nations.

Fourth, we must renew our commitment to quality teaching. Although the terminology has changed from the 1990s to 2016, from *key competencies* to *21st century skills* to *new pedagogies*, the essence of quality teaching remains the same.

Fifth, we must have consistent feedback for teachers and leaders at every level. In Australia, feedback is a mandatory process, including conversations between teachers and leaders at least twice a year. These are goal-oriented conversations that take place everywhere from the class-room to the Ministry of Education.

Sixth and finally, change leadership depends on a core focus on common goals. Unfortunately, there are few examples in schools where sustained change has occurred. Even the most promising international examples have lasted only a few years. Long-term sustainable change in education remains elusive.

When education leaders search for actions with the highest impact, they should first identify those that have low impact or even counterproductive impact on student achievement. In particular, they must avoid those actions that divert teachers and education leaders away from the essential mission and vision of the organization. Education leaders and policymakers often challenge me by asking, "Well, what do we throw out?" The following list is a good start:

▸ Throw out any initiative that would fit into the Weed quadrant of figure 3.3 (page 39)—that is, low implementation and low impact. For example, I have seen more than one school relegate computers to the corner of the library, while the school and district continue to pay for annual premiums and subscriptions to programs that students never use. This is an easy call for leaders—examine every subscription, whether on paper or on the web. Examine actual student and teacher usage, and cancel those that have minimal impact.

▸ Examine worksheets used as homework in the classroom. No classroom visit is complete without examining the file cabinet that contains daily and periodic assessments. You can make a tremendous impact across the school and entire system if you find just one in every classroom that you and the teacher agree is expendable.

▸ Eliminate every meeting (or parts of meetings) whose only purpose is to disseminate information. Other effective ways to disseminate information include emails, social media, Twitter, texts, and so on. Voxer (voxer.com), for example, allows video and audio announcements to be distributed to a wide audience. At the writing of this book, more and more technology tools will become available to help schools communicate quickly and effectively.

- ▶ Eliminate instructional units unrelated to the essential knowledge and skills students need. This requires that teachers engage in a collaborative process to identify these essentials and forge a professional consensus that mastery of the essentials is superior to coverage of nonessentials.

- ▶ Eliminate every process for data entry that could either be automated or delegated to noncertified staff members, giving teachers and administrators time to analyze and act on data rather than merely manipulate it.

- ▶ Eliminate any teaching observation that is not immediately followed by constructive feedback designed to improve instruction.

- ▶ Eliminate conversations that are focused on venting, complaining, or otherwise wasting time on matters that do not lead to improved decisions and results.

In *Leverage Leadership*, Paul Bambrick-Santoyo (2012) provides compelling evidence of schools that, despite having student populations facing extreme poverty, scored better than more than 90 percent of schools in the United States. Bambrick-Santoyo is clear that neither the teachers nor administrators are miracle workers, but that they make the most of every single minute of time in school. They are focused.

Leaders lose their leverage when they are firefighters rather than instructional leaders. They fritter their time away with ceremonial parades, walking around classrooms and schools without providing specific feedback directly to teachers. They drag their heels because they believe the myth that change takes so many years that an immediate impact on results is not possible. It doesn't have to be this way.

Just as Bambrick-Santoyo and other leaders have discovered, you can identify and focus on fewer initiatives and strategies that have greater leverage over student results. Although some of these levers may change from one school system to another, one is universal—the power of effective feedback. This is the subject of the next chapter.

CHAPTER 5

FEEDBACK

The previous chapter identified feedback as a particularly high-leverage strategy to improve student achievement. The same is true of feedback that leaders provide to their colleagues. The same rules apply in both cases—effective feedback is FAST—fair, accurate, specific, and timely (Reeves, 2016). This chapter explores how feedback can succeed and how it can be undermined. It is important that leaders not only give effective feedback but devise methods to receive it as well.

Why Feedback Matters

Hattie and Yates (2014) identify feedback as "one of the most powerful factors implicated in academic learning and resultant achievement" (p. 68). The same is true of teachers and leaders whose professional learning depends not merely on information delivery but on feedback that improves their teaching and leadership. As Kouzes and Posner (2011) suggest:

> With clear goals and detailed feedback, people can become self-correcting and can more easily understand their place in the big picture. With feedback, they can also determine what help they need from others and who might be able to benefit from their assistance. . . . When there is no feedback, production will be less efficient and will exact a significant toll in the form of increased levels of stress and anxiety.

Feedback is at the center of any learning process. For example, consider what happens to your self-confidence without feedback. . . . Without feedback, there is no learning—it's the only way for you to know whether or not you're getting close to your goal and whether or not you're executing properly. Feedback can be embarrassing, even painful. While most people realize intellectually that feedback is a necessary component of self-reflection and growth, they are often reluctant to make themselves open to it. They want to look good more than they want to get good. Researchers consistently point out that the development of expertise or mastery requires one to receive constructive, even critical, feedback. (pp. 282–284)

Just handing out any feedback is not sufficient to improve student performance. The *kind* of feedback matters enormously. Neither excessive praise nor continuous criticism work very well as a form of feedback. In fact, both can discourage students. The next section discusses the kind of feedback that works best for both young and adult students.

Essentials of Effective Feedback

Humans crave feedback on how to improve. In schools, feedback directed toward achieving goals must meet certain characteristics. It must be FAST—fair, accurate, specific, and timely (Hattie & Yates, 2014; Reeves, 2016).

Fair

People often ask me, "How can we determine fairness?" It seems a quandary in the classroom, but it is clear as a bell on the playground. Listen to students explaining the rules of a game. "You can go *here*, but you can't go *there*. You can do *this*, but you can't do *that*." When everyone knows the rules of a game, play ensues and everyone has a good time. When the rules of the game are mysterious and ever-changing, conflict ensues. The same is true in the classroom for both students and adults. When a teacher gives students mysterious and unproductive feedback, the "game" of school is not worth playing. Similarly, when leaders and policymakers provide mysterious and unproductive feedback, teachers often feel like they want to stop playing the "game" of education (Reeves, 2015a).

Fairness need not be mysterious. It's all about consistency. When a student, teacher, or leader behaves in a particular manner, his or her behavior can be judged fairly if a large percentage of observers—typically 80 percent or more—evaluates the behavior in the same way (Bogartz, n.d.).

This happens regularly in classrooms with performance assessments in which the rubrics are so clear that even teachers who are unfamiliar with individual students can evaluate their work in a remarkably consistent manner.

Accurate

Accurate feedback matches the evaluation with what is being evaluated. For example, if you are evaluating a student's proficiency in mathematics, then your evaluation should reflect *only* the student's proficiency in mathematics. This may sound obvious, but a student's grade in mathematics might include many other factors, including attitude, participation, attendance, homework completion, and more. Similarly, when an administrator is assessing a teacher's effectiveness, the primary indication of effectiveness should be student learning. Effective teachers show evidence that students learn more as a result of their instruction. Yet many teacher evaluations focus on classroom displays, lesson plan formats, meeting participation, and other factors that are far afield from the central question: Did students learn as a result of this teacher's instruction?

Specific

When leaders are equipped with evaluation rubrics that are clear and specific, they can evaluate teacher performance with consistency. Kim Marshall (2014) provides some of the best examples of consistent evaluation rubrics for teachers, and Reeves (2009a) does the same for leaders. These are so specific that a group of observers, including veteran teachers, administrators, and those new to the field, could observe the performance of teachers and leaders and come to very similar conclusions. These rubrics, unlike many commercial versions, are free and available for duplication and use. You may visit **go.SolutionTree.com /leadership** to download reproducibles of the sample "Teacher Evaluation Rubrics" and the "Leadership Performance Rubrics." Visit *The Marshall Memo* (www.MarshallMemo.com) to download the full "Teacher Evaluation Rubrics."

A striking feature of both of these rubrics is their clarity and specificity. Marshall deliberately leaves very little space for notes. Observers can make the most efficient use of the rubrics by simply highlighting what they see, not what they don't see. It is therefore possible to express nuance that is far more valuable than, "You are a Level 3."

Instead, each observation provides objective and consistent information about what the observer saw as well as a clear path toward improvement. If the observation reveals that the teacher is a Level 2 in an area of classroom management, then there is a clear path to move to the next level. The same is true of leadership assessment, which is entirely based on objective observation.

This level of specificity offers two advantages. First, observations of each teacher and leader can be consistent. Even when observers see the same behavior, the notes they record can vary. By contrast, highlighting phrases in the rubric gives precisely the same observation and feedback to each teacher and leader. Second, because the feedback is part of a performance continuum, teachers have a clear map to progress to the next level. Ineffective evaluations simply tell teachers what they did wrong or give vague praise about their enthusiasm and classroom control. Effective feedback is explicit and constructive, providing the same map for teachers that great scoring rubrics provide for students. Feedback is not, in these contexts, merely an evaluation but an essential guide to improved performance.

Timely

Can you imagine if Olympic officials observed athletes, noted their scores, and then mailed their decisions weeks after the competition? That is as counterproductive as evaluation systems whose timing between observation and feedback is more than a month (New York City Department of Education, 2015). If feedback is to impact performance, it must be immediate.

Teachers should provide feedback *in class*. Some of their most valuable time is spent providing feedback to individual students and then observing how the students use that feedback to improve performance. The sooner outcomes are known and articulated through objective measures or assignments, the more students can focus on achieving them (Hattie & Yates, 2014).

Hattie and Yates (2014) conclude the following about effective feedback:

> Receiving appropriate feedback is incredibly empowering. Why? Because it enables the individual to move forward, to plot, plan, adjust, rethink, and thus exercise self-regulation in realistic and balanced ways. This mental process view of feedback brings with it an important caveat. Feedback works because the goal is known and accurately defined through realistic assessment. This is why assessments become vital in all forms of teaching and formal instruction. (p. 66)

The same is true of feedback for adults. Too often, leaders elevate the feedback they receive on one part of their duties (such as the construction of a plan that will meet district and state requirements) over the imperatives of instructional leadership at the school site.

Principals and other school leaders can provide timely feedback to teachers after an observation—during the next break, for example, and certainly within the same day. Administrators can receive feedback at the end of every meeting, immediately assessing how successfully they met objectives. Just as great teachers collect exit tickets, which check students' understanding and engagement, administrators can collect immediate, specific feedback after every meeting. If a meeting is worth an hour for twenty staff members, then surely it's worth five minutes to assess that time's effectiveness.

Focus, Monitoring, and Efficacy

Schools with high levels of focus, monitoring, and efficacy perform dramatically better than schools that do not have these qualities (Reeves, 2011). But in my research, I found that even schools that claimed to be focused scattered their time and attention over dozens of priorities. While most schools claim to be good at monitoring, they are truly only effective at tracking student test scores. Without monitoring the specific elements of teaching and leadership, leaders will continue to struggle to understand how teaching and learning fit together.

Efficacy sounds like a wonderful quality, but claims of efficacy often give way to a different reality when you ask, "What causes achievement in your school?" If the teachers and school leaders reply that student achievement is mostly related to teaching and leadership, then we know the school's teachers and leaders are exhibiting high levels of efficacy—that is, they believe that they influence student results. But if the reply points to factors *outside* of their control—student home life, language, socioeconomic status—then it becomes clear that these teachers and school leaders lack efficacy because they believe that student performance is out of their realm of influence. In these situations, schools often cling to administrative compliance. However bad student results may be, school leaders can claim that they followed instructions, complied with format requirements, and produced the necessary documents.

Although conformity with plan format requirements is not related to student achievement over the course of three years, three critical variables are strongly associated with improved achievement: (1) focus, (2) monitoring, and (3) efficacy (Reeves, 2011).

By *focus*, I mean that the leader has six or fewer priorities that he or she and teachers regularly discuss and monitor. Contrast this number to the scores, even hundreds, of priorities that many school and system plans express.

By *monitoring*, I mean the monitoring of adult actions. As Gawande (2007) suggests, professional performance is subject to objective observation and measurement. If that is true in the operating suite, then it is also true in the executive suite of the school system. We can count, measure, and be accountable for the adult actions related to student achievement.

Efficacy is perhaps the most important issue for leaders and teachers to address. Efficacy is the bone-deep belief that our work makes a difference. It is not the conviction that other variables are unimportant but rather that, along with demographics and other factors beyond our control, we matter in the lives of students.

One useful exercise is to draw two columns on a piece of paper, with the first column labeled *Things we cannot control* and the second column labeled *Things we can control*. It is necessary to do this exercise more than once. When I poll teachers, an astonishingly high number of them claim that hardly anything is within their control. They claim that every minute of the day is scripted, the schedule is set, and there is almost no part of their day when they can exercise any control. In brief, they lack efficacy.

In surveys of more than two thousand teachers from more than sixty school systems (Reeves, 2006a), I asked about perceptions of decision making in their schools. I defined Level 1 as teacher discretion, Level 2 as collaborative decision making, and Level 3 as unilateral administrative decisions. The teachers' perceptions were startling.

- ▶ **Level 1:** Teacher discretion—4 percent
- ▶ **Level 2:** Collaborative decision making—22 percent
- ▶ **Level 3:** Unilateral administrative decisions—74 percent

Then I did an interesting experiment. I asked the same teachers to list decisions within each of the three categories. So rather than speculating about who controlled decision making in their school, the respondents focused on decisions they had actually made. The results were stunningly different.

▸ **Level 1:** Teacher discretion—39 percent

▸ **Level 2:** Collaborative decision making—34 percent

▸ **Level 3:** Unilateral administrative decisions—27 percent

These data suggest that while school leaders must make some unilateral decisions, these decisions are substantially fewer than perceived by the teachers. Therefore, it is vital that leaders specify the nature of every leadership decision that they make.

Level 1: Teacher Discretion

For Level 1, the leader might say, "Here is the goal we agreed on. I completely trust you to choose the methods to achieve that goal, even if there are differences among us. All I ask is that you let me know your choices so that we can all learn from your professional practices."

Level 2: Collaborative Decision Making

For Level 2, the leader might say, "I'm not going to make this decision, but I need to rely on you to collaborate, consider the pros and cons of each alternative, and then as a group, come to the best decision you can. It will be your decision, not mine."

Level 3: Unilateral Administrative Decisions

Finally, for Level 3 decisions, the leader might say, "This is one of those times when I must make the call. I try to limit leadership decisions to what I might call 'safety and value' decisions. If it's a matter of safety for staff or students, or if it's a matter of being true to our values, then occasionally—but not very often—I must make the call. Even if you disagree with it, I need to ask you to support it."

Collaboration between leaders and school staff is essential when making most decisions. Consider better ways for describing how to spend collaborative time. You can evaluate every meeting with the group using a simple scoring rubric such as the following. It provides quick feedback to the group regarding the relationship between their espoused norms and their actual performance.

Not meeting standards:

▸ Establishes a leader-focused meeting with little or no deliberation

▸ Allows discussions to be dominated by one or a few

▸ Disempowers teachers to make a difference in student learning

▸ Focuses problems on students and parents

▸ Allows meetings to occur without an agenda

Progressing:

▸ Allows participants to deviate from the agenda

▸ Allows only a few participants to contribute to teaching and learning discussions

▸ Includes some review of student work to guide evidence-based discussions

▸ Establishes norms but does not maintain them

Proficient:

▸ Creates weekly structure without micromanagement

▸ Asks follow-up questions

▸ Shares instructional strategies

▸ Examines data and correlation to professional practices

▸ Establishes and maintains norms, including active participation by all members

▸ Focuses on learning by students and teachers, what adults can do differently to improve learning, and evidence-based discussions tied to solutions

▸ Distributes leadership so that everyone's voice is honored

▸ Responds to priorities that arise in meetings

▸ Uses clear agendas that contain a common understanding of participant expectations

▸ Establishes the context of the meeting and how it relates to previous and future meetings

An exemplary leader meets all the standards of a proficient leader, as well as:

▸ Includes instructional leadership at each meeting that provides coaching and support to progress dialogue and meet outcomes

▸ Examines formative data weekly

▸ Creates opportunities for just-in-time professional development

▸ Focuses on a continuous growth model to include student learning objectives, professional practice goals, and the district's mission

It is important to recall some fundamental rules about rubrics. First, when applying rubrics to human performance, whether for adults or children, the enemy is not other evaluators; the enemy is ambiguity. Therefore, if the preceding rubric, or any of the other rubrics listed in this book, doesn't work for you or your team, then please change it. Second, the fundamental purpose of any feedback system is to improve performance. It's not an evaluation; it's a roadmap to allow teachers and leaders at every level to candidly acknowledge where they are, and then use that feedback to get to the next level of performance.

When Feedback Goes Wrong

Just as a good rubric explains exemplary as well as substandard performance, we must do the same for leadership feedback. The antonym of the acronym *FAST* is useful here. We know that effective feedback is fair, accurate, specific, and timely. Therefore, getting feedback wrong is a combination of these qualities: unfair, inaccurate, ambiguous, and delayed. No neat mnemonic devices here, but the following represents a rubric that leaders might consider when they give feedback to their colleagues and, for that matter, when they give feedback to themselves.

Leadership can be an incredibly lonely position, with unremitting demands twenty-four hours a day. The evaluation rubrics used for leaders can run scores of pages and seem like a catalog of expectations. The same is true for contemporary teacher evaluations. The sheer quantity of characteristics and actions that they are supposed to demonstrate can be overwhelming. But for now, I'll focus on one of the most significant elements of leadership performance—feedback. We should expect the same qualities of teachers and leaders when it comes to giving effective feedback.

▸ **Exemplary:** Feedback focuses explicitly on observed performance, not intentions. The feedback is so specific and clear that different observers with various backgrounds and titles can observe the same teacher or leader's professional practices and come to very similar conclusions. It is the teacher's actual professional practices—not the opinions of any of the observers—that matter, because the observation rubric is so explicit. Observers can attribute no consistent discrepancies in their reviews to gender, ethnicity, sexual orientation or identity, age, or any other variable except the teacher or leader's actual professional practices. They do not average their accumulated observations but rather make a professional determination about the teacher or leader's performance at the end of the year based on his or her response to feedback and improved performance.

▶ **Proficient:** Feedback is fair, accurate, specific, and timely. It conforms to the requirements of the evaluation and observation guidelines of state and district requirements. There is occasional informal feedback, but its primary focus is compliance with the evaluation system. Sometimes administrators ask teachers and leaders to evaluate themselves in order to save time. This also lessens conflict with the staff and union and speeds paperwork.

▶ **Progressing:** Feedback is rare, and when it does occur, it is vague and inconsistent. It mostly consists of phrases such as, "Good job!" and the teachers and leaders receiving this accolade having no idea what it means. When they receive real evaluations, often without consultation or discussion, it is a surprise. This leads to conflict and uncertainty. There is bare compliance with external directives on accountability and evaluation, but little impact on teacher and leader performance.

▶ **Not meeting standards:** The evaluations are grossly unfair—that is, two different teachers or leaders with the same performance can receive vastly different evaluations based largely on the evaluator's personal relationships with them. There is little or no relationship between the observation rubric and actual performance. The comments are so vague that those being evaluated have no idea how to improve, and the performance under review appears not to have improved over the past several years. Teachers typically receive evaluations at the end of the year—sometimes after the school year is over—so they have no immediate opportunity to use feedback to improve their performance.

When Feedback Is Right

The FAST principle applies at every level, from the boardroom to the classroom. Superintendents should not receive evaluations at the end of their contracts;

instead, they should get feedback every month, using specific criteria established before the superintendent signed a contract.

One of the most important innovations leaders can introduce into the superintendent hiring process is leadership performance rubrics, similar to those available at **go.SolutionTree.com/leadership**, for the incoming superintendent. Board members should agree on more than salary and benefits. They also should agree on their specific expectations for the new superintendent, the method they will use to evaluate him or her, and the degree to which those expectations are or are not met.

In an ideal world, the board also would establish a system for self-accountability, measuring and displaying the extent to which it met its policy leadership goals. For example, the board could quantify the amount of meeting time devoted to deliberation compared to presentations. This doesn't deny the importance of time spent addressing public comments and questions and other instances in which the board simply sits and listens. But time is a zero-sum game—every minute spent listening to a presentation that could have gone out by email is a minute not devoted to deliberation and questions. Time allocation is something the board should determine and for which it should be accountable.

A second example of board accountability is its decision-making process. Ideally, the board should always consider a choice between mutually exclusive alternatives. The most common practice is for the board to consider a single alternative at a time for an up or down vote. But the best practice in leadership is an environment in which, with great respect and consideration, the board engages in discussion and debate regarding a selection of alternatives. This requires the superintendent and cabinet to change the practice of subordinating dissent about a choice.

The practice of deliberating on mutually exclusive alternatives means policymakers find advantages and disadvantages of each alternative. Where there is unanimity, the superintendent and board chair are wise to assign senior leaders and board members to take an opposing view. This may be awkward at first for a board or cabinet that does not consider debate and dissent part of the culture. But it is imperative to improve the quality of decision making. Consider the number of multimillion-dollar technology decisions in the past few years, preceded by a presentation, a recommendation by the staff, and then a decision by the board. How many bad decisions might have been avoided with a culture of discussion and debate?

We must depart from the notion that feedback is uncomfortable and evaluative. Perhaps this feeling stems from the most uncomfortable experience of many employees—their annual performance review. It violates every FAST principal. It is neither fair nor accurate (two employees with similar performances receive different ratings). It's not specific ("You're a three, and that's what we give most people" provides little direction for improvement), and it's not timely. The typical end-of-year review also includes salary and promotion decisions, so there is no opportunity for the employee to respond to feedback and seek improvement—at least until the same fruitless process repeats twelve months later.

Imagine that you are at an anniversary dinner with your spouse, and you say, "Before we start this dinner, I'd like to give you your annual performance review." I wouldn't expect that celebration to go particularly well. Nevertheless, leaders who would never evaluate their spouses (at least not during an anniversary dinner) don't hesitate to use this very practice with employees.

The fundamental message of this chapter is that people thrive on feedback—provided that the feedback is fair, accurate, specific, and timely. The same is true of students. Contrary to popular myth, students don't need grades to motivate them—but feedback is absolutely crucial to improving their performance. If we expect leaders and everyone else on the staff to improve, we must first establish a culture in which there is room for improvement. That is, both individuals and institutions must be willing to change. That is the greatest challenge we must face and the subject of our next chapter.

CHAPTER 6

CHANGE

Change is pervasive in our lives, and education leaders face more than their fair share. National and local policies in the United States move with the political winds and often impose these changes. Between 2008 and 2016, the United Kingdom, Australia, Canada, and the United States have been buffeted by changes in national policies that influenced curriculum, assessment, teacher evaluation, and inevitably, education leadership. Too often, however, external interests demand change and leaders don't assess whether systems are ready. In this chapter, I provide a simple tool, the Change Readiness Assessment, that can help leaders and everyone else in the system determine the extent to which they are ready for change. Finally, we consider historical claims about systemic change and evaluate them in light of the best research on the subject.

Costs and Benefits of Change

Before you begin work with a group or an entire system that might involve change, consider the simple question, What are the costs and benefits of change, considering the short-term and long-term impacts? The chart in figure 6.1 (page 80) can help educators analyze these costs and benefits.

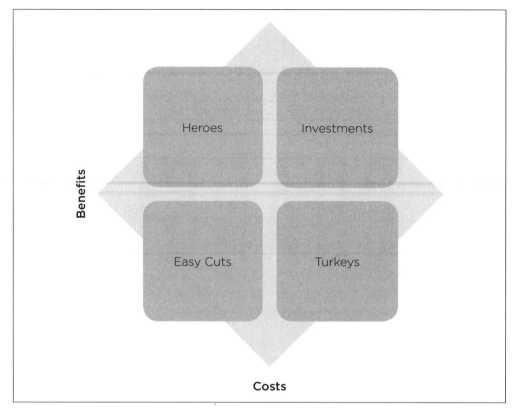

Figure 6.1: Costs and benefits of change.

Change is only worth deliberating if its proponents recognize the costs involved, and if its opponents recognize the benefits. Both sides do not need to begin the deliberations by agreeing with one another, but they must consider the points of view of the individuals in the entire group to get beyond the hardening of positions that typically accompanies group deliberations.

While it has been many years since Covey (1989) popularized the statement "Seek first to understand, then to be understood," many group deliberations begin in precisely the opposite manner. The position of the group leader is clear before the meeting, and the purpose of deliberations is not to understand alternative points of view but to seek buy-in from group participants. This procedure guarantees the illusion of assent, pushing dissent from the meeting into the parking lot. The group replaces rigorous deliberations with a display of happy talk, with leaders absorbed in self-admiration for their persuasive abilities and opponents absorbed in resentment at not being heard, understood, or respected.

Easy Cuts

The lower-left quadrant of figure 6.1, Easy Cuts, is simple, involving changes with low benefits and low costs. These are the detritus of long-gone change initiatives that can be swept out with the trash. The other three quadrants, however, are much more difficult to dismiss.

Turkeys

The lower-right quadrant, Turkeys, represents high-cost, low-benefit programs that live on forever. These are the most expensive initiatives recommended by senior leaders, supported by a visible vendor, and willingly funded by the board. Among these are technology initiatives of which, as Fullan (2014) documents, only a fraction of students use for collaboration, model building, and exploration, while the vast majority of students use for information retrieval. They might as well have as their only technology a sheaf of paper, a number-two pencil, and the 1960s *Encyclopedia Britannica*. It's actually worse than that, because the *Encyclopedia Britannica* had some critical reasoning that went into its creation that filtered out most of the bad content, while students who pursue an answer on the web could find anything from accurate responses to politically charged hate speech.

The Turkeys quadrant also contains some of the most expensive and least productive professional development initiatives. Although a few professional development programs are strongly associated with gains in student achievement (as previous chapters demonstrated, nonfiction writing, PLCs, and effective feedback meet this standard), many involve only the transmission of information. Many are politically tinged with the implicit threat that failure to adopt them would constitute a contradiction of the system's basic values. These proposals are ideal opportunities for the board to insist on the mutually exclusive decision discipline—that is, to make sure and hear the arguments for and against the proposed professional development program.

It is never comfortable to argue the opposing side of a proposed initiative that is politically popular, but these arguments are essential for successful decision making. The Turkeys quadrant—high cost, low benefit—is the greatest leadership quandary. I have learned that every turkey has a champion; and thus, someone always promotes even the least productive and most expensive initiatives, including those with powerful political connections. The role of the leader is to place each initiative in the appropriate quadrant and then focus on those with the highest benefit for the education system.

Heroes

It's tough to be a hero when decisions are controversial and changes entail genuine loss. It's easy to be a hero when leaders find high benefits and low-cost opportunities. For example, it costs almost nothing to change the grading scale from a one hundred–point scale to a four-point scale, yet the reduction of failures is astounding (Reeves, 2016). It costs very little to change homework from a meaningless compliance drill to a practice that improves performance. It costs very little to transform board meetings and cabinet meetings into meaningful deliberations rather than affirmations of the perceived desires of administrative leadership, and the benefits of these deliberations can be enormous.

Investments

While the Heroes quadrant of high benefits and low cost would strike many as low-hanging fruit and easily accomplished, the truth is that it's incredibly difficult to persuade people that high-benefit, low-cost initiatives are worth the effort. They become Oscar Wilde's perfect cynics who know "the price of everything but the value of nothing" (Goodreads, n.d.).

They prefer the upper-right quadrant, Investments, in which both the costs and benefits are high. Here we find the rare technology initiative that actually improves student achievement. We might also find the investment in extraordinary teacher and administrator performance.

Teachers in international and public schools in Hong Kong, Singapore, Korea, and elsewhere might earn twice or three times the salary of other countries' college graduates in different professions (DuFour, 2015a). This notion is alien in the United States, where the best teachers remain on the same salary scale as the worst teachers. Even the mention of *best* and *worst* is antithetical to the tone of discussions in some international education circles.

However, investing in making teaching an attractive, esteemed profession would be staggering, as DuFour (2015a) suggests in his landmark book *In Praise of American Educators*. Critics of American education often express the desire to make American education more like that in Finland or Korea, but they do not recognize the investment those countries make in teaching and education leadership professions. Those countries, and others like them, commit to elevating educators, from the earliest days of college through the end of their education careers. Teachers are uniformly high quality because before they ever set foot in a classroom, they have endured a rigorous selection and training process. DuFour (2015a) reports a trend in the United States toward diminishing our investment in teaching. Some states have asked that teachers only pass a background check and sit in a six-week seminar before entering the classroom.

This wide variation in teaching quality explains why administrators are inundated with requests from parents to get the best teachers for their children. It is interesting that in the United States there has been no problem in paying superintendents superior salaries for, the board presumes, superior work—often hundreds of thousands of dollars. This is a pittance compared to the compensation of CEOs who manage billion-dollar budgets and have responsibility for thousands of employees. Nevertheless, it is an interesting contradiction that the salaries and benefits for superintendents have exploded, while those for teachers, including the superstar teachers, have remained relatively low.

Change Readiness Assessments

Mike Wasta is the former superintendent of the school district in Bristol, Connecticut, where he helped make his district the first urban district in Connecticut to achieve adequate yearly progress. Since then, he has been a state and national leader in applying data to improve leadership decision making. Wasta is the creator of the Organizational Change Readiness Assessment, shown in figure 6.2, a tool that any leader can use to assess readiness for systemic change. The Organizational Change Readiness Assessment considers the capacity of the organization and the leader to engage in significant change.

Organizational Change	1	2	3
Planning: The plan was clear, detailed, and effectively communicated.			
Sense of Urgency: There was a widespread sense of immediate need for change.			

Figure 6.2: Organizational change readiness assessment. continued ➡

Organizational Change	1	2	3
Stakeholder Support: Employees, clients, and community understood and supported the change.			
Leadership Focus: Senior leadership made the change their clear and consistent focus long after initiation.			
Impact on Results: The change had a measurable and significant impact on results.			
Total for change 1: _____ Total for change 2: _____ Total for change 3: _____ Total for the two highest changes: _____			

Source: Mike Wasta, 2009. Used with permission.

To use this assessment, consider the degree to which your organization engaged in significant change in the past several years. Then, for each change, identify, on a scale of zero to ten, the degree to which you were ready for change. Ten is the highest possible score, and zero represents a complete lack of readiness for change. Evaluate each change based on the following criteria:

▶ **Planning:** Our plans were clear, detailed, and effectively communicated.

▶ **Sense of urgency:** There was a widespread and urgent sense of the immediate need for change.

▶ **Stakeholder support:** Employees, clients, and community members understood and supported the change.

▶ **Leadership focus:** The senior leadership team made the change with a clear and consistent focus, which continued long after its initiation.

▶ **Impact on results:** The change had a measureable and significant impact on results.

It's important to be candid about past change efforts in order to overcome the inevitable cynical reactions, such as, "I've seen two dozen change efforts come and go, and I waited each one of them out until it imploded or lost steam. I can wait this one out too." If this is the history of the education system, then senior leaders need to admit it forthrightly and make their new change efforts substantially different. To do so, the senior leadership team members must honestly examine their own personal change efforts.

Figure 6.3, the Personal Change Readiness Assessment, helps leaders consider personal changes of the past few years, as well as qualities that are directly analogous to organizational change efforts.

Personal Change	1	2	3
Planning: I planned in advance the steps I would take and knew clearly how to make the change.			
Sense of Urgency: I knew that the price of failing to change was much greater than the price of changing.			
Personal Support: My family and friends knew I was making a change and supported me.			
Personal Focus: I devoted time to initiating and maintaining the change despite my busy schedule.			
Impact on Results: I can measure the results of the change, and they are clear and significant.			

Figure 6.3: Personal change readiness assessment.   continued ➡

Total for change 1: _____
Total for change 2: _____
Total for change 3: _____
Total for the two highest changes: _____

Source: Adapted from Reeves, 2009b.

To use this assessment, consider three personal changes you have made in the past five years. These changes could represent strategic or behavioral changes at work, or changes in your personal life, such as an improvement in your diet, exercise routine, or personal relationships. Then, for each change, identify, on a scale of zero to ten, the degree to which you were ready for change. Ten is the highest possible score, and zero represents a complete lack of readiness for change. Evaluate each change based on the following criteria:

▸ **Planning:** I planned in advance the steps I would take and knew clearly how to make the change.

▸ **Sense of urgency:** I knew that the price of failing to change was much greater than the price of changing.

▸ **Personal support:** My family and friends knew I was making a change and supported me.

▸ **Personal focus:** I devoted time to initiating and maintaining the change despite my busy schedule.

▸ **Impact on results:** I can measure the results of the change, and they are clear and significant.

The combination of the Organizational Change Readiness Assessment and the Personal Change Readiness Assessment allows you to plot your results on a two-by-two matrix. This analysis of organizational and personal change allows leaders to plot their present status on four points on the graph in figure 6.4, the Change Readiness Matrix.

The Change Readiness Matrix comprises four levels of readiness for organizational change, based on a combination of personal and organizational change histories: (1) ready for resistance, (2) ready for frustration, (3) ready for learning, and (4) ready for change.

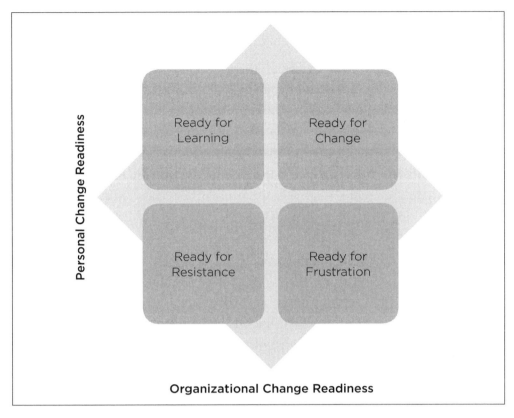

Figure 6.4: Change readiness matrix.

Ready for Resistance

The lower-left quadrant, Ready for Resistance, represents the intersection of low personal and organizational change. The motto of this type of organization could be, "Things are fine just the way they are." You will find lots of blind affirmation without any regard to results.

When neither the leader nor the organization has a history of successful change, then the most likely result of any new change initiative will be resistance, anger, undermining, or simply ignoring the effort. Without stakeholder support or leadership execution, these organizations will simply wait out every new change initiative and the leaders who attempt to implement them.

Ready for Frustration

The lower-right quadrant, Ready for Frustration, represents when the organization is ready and eager for change, but the leader is reluctant, perhaps for political reasons, to engage in it. This often happens when teaching and administrative staff members are ready for change, but the superintendent and board, influenced by a reluctant community, are not yet willing to make the leap.

When an organization with a strong history of change is led by someone who is either reluctant to engage in systemic change or who lacks the personal capacity to do so, then there is a strong potential for frustration. Each time the organization gets ahead of the leader, and the ensuing change fails to be supported by senior leadership, change becomes less safe. Eventually, the organization stops taking the risks and migrates to the left side of the matrix, Resistance. In this quadrant, there is neither an individual nor organizational readiness for change. Fear replaces hope and doubt replaces optimism. The next leader will inherit an organization with severely compromised change readiness, and it will take time to rebuild trust and regain change capacity.

Ready for Learning

The upper-left quadrant, Ready for Learning, represents a high degree of personal change and a low degree of organizational change. This is typical of a new leader brought into an organization with a mandate for change. While the leader is willing and eager for change, the organizational enthusiasm for change may lag far behind.

The leader demonstrates a history of successful change, with a strong capacity for planning and executing change. The organization can learn from the leader's personal and professional example. Before undertaking a new change initiative, however, the leader must attend to the learning needs of the organization. Specifically, the organization may need work on planning, communicating, and executing change. Moreover, the organization must create an evidence-based culture in which a clear and compelling case for change leads to a sense of urgency by every stakeholder. Finally, a commitment to clear and public data displays must be in place so that the results of the change can be widely shared, reinforcing the commitment and hard work of every person contributing to the change effort.

Ready for Change

The upper-right quadrant, Ready for Change, represents the ideal intersection of high degrees of personal and organizational change. Both the leaders and the organization understand what change requires, and they have the experience and desire to make the changes.

When both the leader and the organization have exceptional change capacity, it is a model of resilience. This organization can adapt to environmental and cultural shifts, change strategies and form, innovate in services and resources, and create an atmosphere of excitement and engagement.

Claims About Change

There is no scarcity of claims about change. It's the only constant, as per the cliché. But while claims are abundant, evidence is scarce. Consider each of the following common claims about change leadership and consider how you might challenge it:

▸ Systemic change takes five to seven years to be fully implemented.

▸ When you initiate a change, implementation dips are inevitable. Expect results to get worse before they get better.

▸ In order to make effective changes, strategic planning is essential.

▸ Vision statements bring the system together.

▸ Before making important changes, it is imperative to gain buy-in from the entire staff.

▸ Do the important, not the urgent. That is, don't get too focused on urgent priorities. Step back and focus on the long-term important goals.

Each of these claims sounds reasonable, and they have certainly gained credibility with incessant repetition. The only problem is that they all lead down the wrong path. Let's consider each claim in turn and contrast the prevailing wisdom with an alternative viewpoint.

Systemic Change Takes Five to Seven Years

The first claim is that systemic change always takes five to seven years. It is entirely possible that, looking in the rearview mirror, some changes have taken this long. But consider other systemic changes that have resulted in profound shifts in a much shorter period of time. When the Cardinal Community School District in Iowa implemented the "ketchup room," which requires students to catch up with their homework every Friday, it resulted in a more than 90 percent decline in student failures, a more than 50 percent reduction in suspensions, and an increase in student attendance (Reeves, 2012, 2016).

These changes were accomplished in a single year. Three years after the initial implementation, Superintendent Joel Pedersen reports that the results continue to improve, even as the percentage of students from low-income and English-learning (EL) families continues to increase (J. Pedersen, personal communication, August 31, 2015).

Other changes can have an equally profound impact in a short period of time. For example, when teachers and administrators change their grading system from a one hundred–point scale to a four-point scale, they dramatically reduce the impact of a zero and the frequency of course failures. This kind of grading reform is easier than most to implement and does not require a significant amount of effort by the staff. Consider two students with identical grades in each of these two systems. The following example demonstrates this point clearly (Reeves, 2015a):

One hundred–point scale:

- ▸ 90 = A
- ▸ 80 = B
- ▸ 70 = C
- ▸ 60 = D
- ▸ Missing assignments = 0

Four-point scale:

- ▸ 4 = A
- ▸ 3 = B
- ▸ 2 = C
- ▸ 1 = D
- ▸ Missing assignments = 0

The following two students have identical records:

- ▸ **Student A:** 90, 80, 0, 0, 80, 90, 0, 70, 80, 90
- ▸ **Student B:** 4, 3, 0, 0, 3, 4, 0, 2, 3, 4

Student A's average grade is 58, a solid F. Student B's average grade is 2.3, a C. If neither student were evaluated using the average, both would have a final grade of A.

The simple act of changing the scale from one hundred points to four points, and substituting the teacher's professional judgment instead of the average as the mechanism for determining the final score, dramatically lowers failure rates. It doesn't take five to seven years. It doesn't take a single year. These changes can take place in a single semester.

The same is true of teacher and administrator evaluations. The simple step of eliminating the average and substituting administrators' professional judgment might save the careers of teachers who took the feedback they received in the fall, used it diligently, and finished in the springtime with high levels of performance unburdened by false starts in the beginning.

Implementation Dips Are Inevitable

The next common claim about change leadership is that when you initiate a change, implementation dips are inevitable—expect results to get worse before they get better. Fullan observed the persistence of implementation dips in his 2001 book *Leading in a Culture of Change*. I asked Fullan about this and other quotes attributed (and often misattributed) to him, and he explained, "I've learned a lot about change in the past fifteen years!" He went on to suggest that as his studies expand globally, we have learned enough about systemic change to accelerate and improve the impact of effective leadership (M. Fullan, personal communication, September 20, 2014).

While it is true that changes in test formats and content can lead to dips in student performance, it is not true of *every* change initiative. A cynic might suggest that the implementation dip is the last refuge of consultants who recommend changes that promised improvement but who are unwilling to stick around to see those promises come to fruition. In fact, change initiatives can and should yield positive results in both the short and long term. Indeed, to sustain long-term implementation, it is essential that change leaders achieve some short-term wins to gain the trust and confidence of the people who are responsible for securing long-term change implementation.

Strategic Planning Is Essential

The next claim is that in order to make effective changes, strategic planning is essential. It is important for organizations to separate *strategic planning* from *strategic planners*. The former can be a guiding light for educational systems, while the latter can create multiple roadblocks to meaningful change. The best strategic plans link mission, vision, values, strategies, and action plans seamlessly in a focused way.

Unfortunately, strategic planners are rarely paid for their brevity and focus. Typical strategic planning documents include action plans that are hundreds of pages long, even for a small school system. The strategic planning objectives and the documents associated with them reflect a relentless inclusiveness with multiple committees, sometimes numbering into the hundreds of participants. Each committee produces strategies, objectives, and action plans. No one, least of all the strategic planners, suggests that these ideas are overwhelming or unfocused or—worst of all—divert the school system and its leaders from their primary objective of improving student achievement.

Their earnestness is reminiscent of Marzano's reflection on state standards in the 1990s, in which he states that establishing these standards makes perfect sense, as long as we double the number of years children spend in school (Aguilar, 2009). But it is a rare superintendent who will fire the whole committee and say, "No, we just can't do it all, and thanks for your service."

Strategic planners in school systems are somewhat like members of the U.S. Congress who, on the eve of winter break, all take back something of value— government-funded projects, tax breaks for specific local businesses, and so on, to give to their constituents. This system hardly benefits the United States or, in the case of schools, the entire system, but it does make everyone involved feel as if they can return home with a job well done.

Vision Statements Bring the System Together

The next claim is that vision statements will help bring the system together. In chapter 1, we examined the strengths and weaknesses of mission and vision statements. Perhaps the best way to summarize the promise and poison of vision statements is to consider two visual images. The first is a late work of Claude Monet, one of the most popular Impressionist artists. Even the most casual appreciator of art knows well his *Bridge Over a Pond of Water Lilies* at Giverny, painted many times over the years in different seasons. But as Monet aged and his eyesight declined, his images of the lilies and the bridge grew less distinct, to the point that some viewers might find the images unrecognizable. Monet's late work is the visual counterpart of vision statements that are obtuse beyond recognition. They might once have meant something, but in their later forms, no one besides the creators would recognize their meaning and purpose (Thompson, 2007).

Contrast this obscurity with the drawings by Sir Christopher Wren of St. Paul's Cathedral. St. Paul's is a multicultural marvel. It brought together craftsmen from around the world, including people from different cultures speaking different languages. They built this magnificent cathedral not because they learned English but because they understood the vision of this extraordinary architect. Wren's vision was so clear that people from around the world could understand and execute it. It's quite true that leadership vision is important, but vision statements cannot be obscure and inaccessible to all but the committee involved in creating them (Mount, 2011).

The creators of vision statements should approach their task as an architect might—when the architect, like Sir Christopher Wren, must deal with craftsmen who respond not to written commands but to visual images. In brief, try to craft a vision statement without words.

It's Imperative to Gain Buy-In From the Entire Staff

One of the most pernicious claims about change leadership is that before important changes can be made, it is imperative to gain buy-in from the entire staff. This myth is the antithesis of genuine change. There are two rules of buy-in. First, if a leader has buy-in from the entire staff, then the proposed change is insignificant. Meaningful change is usually difficult. Second, if leaders expect significant change and wait for buy-in, then they will be waiting for the next geological era to begin before they are able to implement it.

The appropriate standard for leaders to use is the "health, safety, and values" test. For example, if drinking water were unsafe, leaders would fix the problem and not wait for buy-in from all the stakeholders. If a crosswalk were unsafe, leaders would identify and fix the problem without waiting for buy-in from the motorists who impatiently cross it. If the question were one of values—for example, equal opportunities for low-income and minority students—then the leaders would not wait for the agreement of those who were happy and satisfied with the previous system of education. Leaders would proceed with changes regardless of the level of buy-in.

Changes in grading systems, for example, allow substantially more students to graduate from high school and succeed in college than in the past. Some people are not comfortable with this state of affairs, but that is hardly a reason to halt progress based on the lack of buy-in from the faculty, parents, and community.

As I have told many education leaders, "You can't choose not to be fired, but you can choose to be fired for the right reasons."

This is not a call for dictatorial rule. Leaders can make the vast majority of their decisions through consensus and listening. But when consensus is not possible, it is the responsibility of the leader to make the tough calls. This has been the case from the abandonment of corporal punishment to the implementation of desegregation. Courageous leaders do not seek consensus or buy-in on essential issues that are fundamentally related to the values of their organization. Rather, they require implementation, even when consensus and buy-in remain elusive.

Do the Important, Not the Urgent

The final claim about change leadership is that we must do the important, not the urgent. Covey's (1989) famous Time Management Matrix divided tasks into those that are important and urgent, important and not urgent, urgent and not important, and neither urgent nor important. He observed that people spend an inordinate amount of time on tasks that are urgent but not important, and that we should redirect our energies to those that are important, even if they are not urgent.

Perhaps this creates a false dichotomy for school leaders who have parents to meet, children to care for, and teachers to observe. This does not include the one hundred other tasks before them, including those imposed by district leadership and other governing bodies. In brief, the urgent and important coincide within the same time and space. Leaders can reconcile this dilemma with moment-to-moment prioritization and delegation. They must ask, "If I were unavoidably not in school today, who would carry out these tasks?" Clearly someone would meet with parents, talk with students, and respond to the external demands of the district and higher headquarters.

Leaders must consider a healthy dose of their own mortality—or least their availability—in order to delegate their tasks wisely. It is entirely possible that a classroom teacher or an assistant director in the central office is better equipped to complete the school plan. It is similarly possible that colleagues at every level can respond to parents' and students' needs.

Georgetown Professor Cal Newport (2016), who studied among high-performing computer scientists at MIT, observed in his book *Deep Work* that cognitively demanding jobs, including teaching and leadership, require the ability to engage in complete focus for some periods of time and attention to multiple demands at other times. In the life of a busy school leader, this might mean taking forty-five minutes to close the door, turn off email, and analyze a set of student data. After that forty-five minutes—the amount of time the leader might have been in a meeting—the leader is again accessible to help deal with urgent demands.

Leaders whose responsibility includes changing the practices, behaviors, and culture of schools can only succeed if they are willing to model change themselves. With relative ease, they can talk about how their own practices, behaviors, and cultural beliefs have changed, and they can authentically discuss why those changes were difficult but necessary. Most important, change leaders can learn from the evidence. When you espouse the foundational elements—purpose, trust, focus, leverage, feedback, and change—you are ready to undertake the lifelong challenge of sustainability. What remains? The next chapter explores how great leaders create sustainable systems that rely on ideas and values, not individual personalities.

CHAPTER 7

SUSTAINABILITY

The term *sustainability* is often associated with care for the environment. When we recycle, compost, and conserve natural resources, we contribute to the sustainability of resources to ensure a planet that is safer for generations to come. Similarly, when education leaders think about sustainability, they take actions today that will serve students and communities long after they have retired.

How to Make Leadership Stick

In their landmark book, *Uplifting Leadership*: *How Organizations, Teams, and Communities Raise Performance*, Hargreaves, Boyle, and Harris (2014) identify the key challenge to sustainability:

> Sustainability is often an afterthought of organizational change. It is the unread postscript, the parting shot that nobody hears, the ripened fruit that's already starting to rot before it reaches its market. On the highway of attempted improvement, last-ditch efforts to secure sustainability are often the final truck stop before disappointment and remorse. Sustainability is the thing we think about when all the action has ended, when the good times are over and the money is all but spent. "This has been great," we say, "but how do we keep it going?" (p. 137)

If there is a literary prize for metaphors, surely these authors have won it. Their point is nevertheless essential to the issue of sustainability. The question is, in simplest terms, How do we keep it going? Schools are full of initiatives that failed to address this question. Government and grant-making agencies often institutionalize the lack of sustainability when they offer grants in three-year cycles, imagining that, as if by magic, schools will continue the program without adequate funding.

Indeed, most grant applications include a commitment by the prospective recipient that it will achieve sustainability for a certain number of years after exhausting the grant funding. But it doesn't work that way, as Jenny Lewis testified (see chapter 4, page 55). New terminology and new programs replace the old, as today's enthusiasms displace those of yesterday. The "out with the old, in with the new" philosophy make sense only if each successive year, or even decade, of educational research brings more promising practices.

But a quick perusal of the most comprehensive list of high-impact education initiatives suggests that newer is not always better (Hattie, 2009). Computer-aided instruction, for example, doesn't even make the top rank of influences on student learning, while the time-honored principle of feedback dominates the top rank of those influences. Therefore, what qualifies as sustainable is not necessarily what is new but what has the capacity for endurance.

Leadership that sticks—that has an impact long after the leader has left for another assignment or to retire—is leadership that is not connected in a temporal way to particular programs. Rather, it is leadership that Fullan (2005) describes as an "adaptive challenge" (p. 14). He posits eight elements of sustainability, which are (1) public service with a moral purpose, (2) commitment to changing context at all levels, (3) capacity building through networks, (4) intelligent accountability, (5) deep learning, (6) dual commitment, (7) short- and long-term results, and (8) the use of the long lever of leadership.

With regard to the long lever of leadership, Fullan contends:

> Archimedes said, "Give me a lever long enough and I can change the world." For sustainability, that lever is leadership— a certain kind of new leadership . . . leadership that operates very differently than is the case in the present, that is valued differently by societies seeking greater sustainability, and that helps produce other similar leaders to create a critical mass. This critical mass is the long lever of leadership. If a system is to

be mobilized in the direction of sustainability, leadership at all
levels must be the primary engine. . . . We need a system laced
with leaders who are trained to think in bigger terms and to act
in ways that affect larger parts of the system as a whole. (p. 27)

Pause for a moment to consider how genuinely rare this sort of systems thinking is. In fact, present evaluation systems reward what we might call *anti-systems
thinking*, in which every gain of my part of the system is a loss for your part of the
system, and vice versa. For each school that receives an A by legislative mandate,
another school receives an F. For every teacher who receives the highest rating
and the job security that accompanies it, there are at least a few who receive low
ratings along with financial and professional ruin.

Fullan's (2005) vision that "we need a system laced with leaders who are trained
to think in bigger terms and to act in ways that affect larger parts of the system
as a whole" (p. 27) is possible only when we begin to realize that leadership is not
a zero-sum game in which my gain is your loss. Whether it is the league tables
in the United Kingdom and Australia or the relentless grading systems in North
America, the great philosopher of education in the present environment appears
to be the essayist and short story writer Somerset Maugham, who reportedly
said, "Now that I've grown old, I realize that for most of us it is not enough to
have achieved personal success. One's best friend must also have failed" (Cordell,
1969). In such an environment, we should not be surprised to see collaboration
challenged and destroyed.

The Practice of Effective Leadership

It is essential to transform theory into practice. What specifically can leaders do
right now in order to implement practices that will have both an immediate and
lasting effect on their organizations? There are but three essentials based on the
testimonies and research in the preceding chapters.

Tell the Truth

First, leaders must tell the truth as best they know it. It won't always be perfect,
but staff members will not focus so much on statistical accuracy as they will on
personal honor. Do what you say you will do. Say what you mean. Above all,
don't do what you don't believe in. Followers observe not only what leaders do
but also what they refuse to do.

Focus on the Most Important Priorities

Second, focus your leadership attention on the most important priorities. However ponderous and prolific the good intentions from higher headquarters may be, don't squander all your attention on your colleagues. Focus, not fragmentation, is the essential rule.

Provide Feedback That Is Fair, Accurate, Specific, and Timely

Third and most important, provide feedback that is fair, accurate, specific, and timely. Your colleagues can take it—trust them. Don't sugarcoat it. If you expect change to happen, then deal honestly with people, even when it is unpleasant. And when praise is appropriate, dole it out in heaps—far more than the anemic descriptions in personnel evaluations. Every high-five from the leader is worth dozens of laudatory reviews. Leaders can cheapen personnel reviews by awarding them in a profligate manner. However, the genuine appreciation of a leader is a rare commodity that followers value above any other bureaucratic incentive.

The Day After Leaders Leave

Mortality—or at least our next job—awaits us all. There are only three times when a leader may address the issues of delegation: too early, just right, and too late. The Goldilocks principle demonstrates that "just right" rarely happens, leaving only two choices—too early and too late. Given these parameters, the choice is clear, and wise leaders plan early for delegating the responsibilities of leadership. They allow colleagues to practice and refine their skills, even when such delegation is unnecessary.

Every U.S. president addresses a letter to his or her successor. For generations, these letters have conveyed a peaceful transition from one administration to the next, and a sense that however contentious the elections might have been, there is genuine goodwill among those who hold the reins of power. But why do we wait until there is a designated successor to write such a letter?

As you conclude your reading of this book, consider writing a letter to your successors right now. Express to them your hopes and aspirations. Confide your fears. Share your dreams. Whether you lead a single school, system, state, or nation, write the letter now—long before you need to. May it guide you and your successors long into the future.

APPENDIX

SHADOW A STUDENT

This appendix is reprinted with permission from Authentic Education © 2014.

Purpose: This activity helps leaders and other educators (the shadowers) empathize with students (thus, to see the school through the eyes of students rather than themselves). In so doing, the shadowers come away with insights about the intended and unintended effects of school practices and policies on students. They can then share these insights with colleagues in a constructive way.

Process: As a team, educators shadow individual students in their school or district for a full or half day. Shadowers go to each of their assigned student's classes, stand near the student in the hall between classes, and in general, perceive the school experience through the eyes and ears of the student.

1. Ensure that teachers and administrators at the school in question assent to and are informed about the day of shadowing. Provide this and other Authentic Education handouts describing the day.

2. Identify students who are comfortable being shadowed. (You may need advance help from teachers or administrators at the school to find students.) As a team, try to shadow students in a range of achievement levels. You may wish to practice the exercise before the day of shadowing by visiting a class and casually watching a student.

3. Meet students individually the day before shadowing (or, if necessary, before school starts that morning) to explain the process and prepare for students' schedules on the day of the visit.

4. Shadowers position themselves to be able to watch the student at all times during the school day.

5. Shadowers should try to suspend any and all judgment about what is taking place in class and focus on the experience of being a student—what it feels like physically, emotionally, and intellectually.

    a. How engaged is the shadowed student? How physically active is the student?

    b. How interesting is the class from the student's perspective?

    c. How easy is it to follow the teacher from the student's perspective? Is there a clear goal to the activities? How is the pace? The flow? (Watch the student's face, not the teacher's, to infer this information.)

6. Pay attention to the student's affect/body language/talk as he or she leaves class and heads to the next location: Is he or she still processing? Is he or she immediately onto something else now?

7. Between classes, if possible, have a one-minute debriefing with the student about the high and low points of the class from his or her perspective. Follow up on any of your observations in light of the questions in number 5. Look at any work the student completed, including notes, papers, worksheets, and so on.

8. As the day ends, speak with the student about the high and low points of the day and, especially, whether this day was typical or not.

9. Thank the student and the staff of the visited school.

10. As soon as possible, write key detailed observations—not judgments—about what you saw, heard, and felt over the course of the day: How would you describe this student's day? After you have described the day, jot down discussion questions, topics, and further action research that arise from your experience to propose to colleagues.

11. Debrief at the day's end with other team members and with the visited teachers about what you learned, using the question, What was it like to be a student here today? Shadowers should describe what they saw,

felt, and thought. Visited teachers should then briefly supply context—how typical a class and day was this? Finally, on their own, shadowers discuss any conclusions or recommendations that they would like to bring to the faculty based on their experiences.

REFERENCES AND RESOURCES

Adams, S. (1997, December 7). *Dilbert*. Accessed at http://dilbert.com/strip/1997-12-07 on February 4, 2016.

Aguilar, E. (2009, November 9). *How to focus lessons and learning goals*. Accessed at www.edutopia.org/focus-student-learning-power-standards on February 4, 2016.

Alliance for Excellent Education. (n.d.a). *The crisis & economic potential in America's education system*. Accessed at http://impact.all4ed.org/#crisis/high-school-grad-rates /united-states on March 23, 2015.

Alliance for Excellent Education. (n.d.b). *High school graduation rates*. Accessed at http://all4ed.org/issues/high-school-graduation-rates on February 4, 2016.

American Psychological Association. (2014, April 23). *Employee distrust is pervasive in U.S. workforce*. Accessed at www.apa.org/news/press/releases/2014/04/employee -distrust.aspx on April 1, 2015.

Bambrick-Santoyo, P. (2012). *Leverage leadership: A practical guide to building exceptional schools*. San Francisco: Jossey-Bass.

Bernal, P. (2014, April 3). *The price of everything and the value of nothing*. Accessed at https://paulbernal.wordpress.com/2014/04/13/the-price-of-everything-and-the -value-of-nothing on February 4, 2016.

Blakeman, C. (2012, May 25). *Why most mission statements suck so bad*. Accessed at www.inc.com/chuck-blakeman/why-most-mission-statements-suck-so-bad.html on February 4, 2016.

Bogartz, R. S. (n.d.). *Interrater agreement and combining ratings*. Accessed at http:// people.umass.edu/~bogartz/Interrater%20Agreement.pdf on February 21, 2016.

Brown, P. C., Roediger, H. L., III, & McDaniel, M. A. (2014). *Make it stick: The science of successful learning*. Cambridge, MA: The Belknap Press of Harvard University Press.

Cameron, W. B. (1963). *Informal sociology: A casual introduction to sociological thinking*. New York: Random House.

Carroll, L. (1865). *Alice's adventures in Wonderland*. The Gutenberg Project. Accessed at www.gutenberg.org/files/11/11-h/11-h.htm#link2HCH0006 on February 4, 2016.

Center for Parenting Education. (n.d.). *A case against corporal punishment*. Accessed at http://centerforparentingeducation.org/library-of-articles/discipline-topics/case -corporal-punishment on March 30, 2015.

Cherok, R. J. (2015, June 12). In all things, charity. *Christian Standard*. Accessed at http://christianstandard.com/2015/06/in-all-things-charity on February 4, 2016.

Childress, G. (2014, November 2). Study says high principal turnover costly to nation. *The Herald-Sun*. Accessed at www.heraldsun.com/news/x1476703465/Study-says -high-principal-turnover-costly-to-nation on March 24, 2015.

Congress.gov. (2001). *H.R.1: No Child Left Behind Act of 2001*. Accessed at www .congress.gov/bill/107th-congress/house-bill/1 on February 4, 2016.

Cordell, R. A. (1969). *Somerset Maugham, a writer for all seasons: A biographical and critical study*. Bloomington: Indiana University Press.

Council of Great City Schools (2014, Fall). *Urban school superintendents: Characteristics, tenure, and salary—Eighth survey and report*. Accessed at www .cgcs.org/cms/lib/DC00001581/Centricity/Domain/87/Urban%20Indicator _Superintendent%20Summary%2011514.pdf on February 5, 2016.

Covey, S. R. (1989). *The seven habits of highly effective people: Habit 5—Seek first to understand, then to be understood*. Accessed at www.stephencovey.com/7habits/7habits -habit5.php on April 11, 2016.

Darling-Hammond, L. (2015). *Teaching in the flat world: Learning from high-performing systems*. New York: Teachers College Press.

Darling-Hammond, L., & Ifill-Lynch, O. (2006). If they'd only do their work! *Educational Leadership*, *63*(5), 8–13.

DuFour, R. (2015a). *In praise of American educators: And how they can become even better*. Bloomington, IN: Solution Tree Press.

DuFour, R. (2015b, March). *Leaders wanted: Keys to effective leadership in Professional Learning Communities at Work*. Presentation at the Summit on Professional Learning Communities at Work, Phoenix, AZ.

DuFour, R., DuFour, R., & Eaker, R. (2008). *Revisiting Professional Learning Communities at Work: New insights for improving schools*. Bloomington, IN: Solution Tree Press.

DuFour, R., DuFour, R., Eaker, R., & Many, T. (2010). *Learning by doing: A handbook for Professional Learning Communities at Work* (2nd ed.). Bloomington, IN: Solution Tree Press.

DuFour, R., & Reeves, D. (2016). The futility of PLC lite. *Kappan*, *97*(6), 69–71.

Dweck, C. S. (2006). *Mindset: The new psychology of success*. New York: Random House.

Elmore, R. (2011). *I used to think . . . and now I think . . . : Twenty leading educators reflect on the work of school reform*. Cambridge, MA: Harvard Education Press.

Favaro, K. (2014, May 22). Strategy or culture: Which is more important? *Strategy+business*. Accessed at www.strategy-business.com/media/file/Strategy-or -Culture2.pdf on March 24, 2015.

Fink, D. (in press). *Trust and verify: The real keys to school improvement*. London: Institute of Education Press.

Fullan, M. (2001). *Leading in a culture of change*. San Francisco: Jossey-Bass.

Fullan, M. (2005). *Leadership and sustainability: System thinkers in action*. Thousand Oaks, CA: Corwin Press.

Fullan, M. (2008). *The six secrets of change: What the best leaders do to help their organizations survive and thrive*. San Francisco: Jossey-Bass.

Fullan, M. (2011, April). *Seminar series 204: Choosing the wrong drivers for whole system reform*. East Melbourne, Victoria, Australia: Centre for Strategic Education.

Fullan, M. (2014). *The principal: Three keys to maximizing impact*. San Francisco: Jossey-Bass.

Gallu, S., & Bolte, C. E., Jr. (1970). *Give 'em hell, Harry!* New York: Samuel French.

Gawande, A. (2007). *Better: A surgeon's notes on performance*. New York: Metropolitan Books.

Goodreads. (n.d.) *Lady Windermere's Fan quotes*. Accessed at www.goodreads.com/work /quotes/1897835-lady-windermere-s-fan on February 21, 2016.

Gramophone. (n.d.). *The world's greatest orchestras*. Accessed at www.gramophone.co.uk /editorial/the-world%E2%80%99s-greatest-orchestras on March 28, 2015.

Guskey, T. R. (2014). *On your mark: Challenging the conventions of grading and reporting*. Bloomington, IN: Solution Tree Press.

Hargreaves, A., Boyle, A., & Harris, A. (2014). *Uplifting leadership: How organizations, teams, and communities raise performance*. San Francisco: Jossey-Bass.

Hattie, J. (2009). *Visible learning: A synthesis of over 800 meta-analyses relating to achievement*. New York: Routledge.

Hattie, J. (2012). *Visible learning for teachers: Maximizing impact on learning*. New York: Routledge.

Hattie, J., & Yates, G. C. R. (2014). *Visible learning and the science of how we learn*. New York: Routledge.

Hoerr, T. R. (2014). Principal connection: Authority in an age of distrust. *Educational Leadership, 72*(2), 86–87.

Ingersoll, R. (2007, September). Short on power, long on responsibility. *Educational Leadership, 65*(1), 20–25.

Katzenbach, J., & Leinwand, P. (2015). *Culture eats strategy for breakfast* [Webinar]. Accessed at www.strategyand.pwc.com/media/file/Katzenbach-Center_Webinar _Culture-Eats-Strategy-for-Breakfast.pdf on March 24, 2015.

Kiley, K. (2011). Saying more with less. *Inside Higher Ed*. Accessed at www
.insidehighered.com/news/2011/06/20/colleges_pare_down_mission_statements
_to_stand_out on February 21, 2016.

King, S. (2010). *On writing: A memoir of the craft*. New York: Simon & Schuster.

Kouzes, J. M., & Posner, B. Z. (2011). *Credibility: How leaders gain and lose it, why
people demand it* (2nd ed.). San Francisco: Jossey-Bass.

The Lever. (n.d.). *Archimedes quotations*. Accessed at www.math.nyu.edu/~crorres
/Archimedes/Lever/LeverQuotes.html on February 5, 2016.

MacArthur, C., Graham, S., & Fitzgerald, J. (Eds.). (2008). *Handbook of writing
research*. New York: Guilford Press.

Mann, A., & Harter, J. (2016, January 7). The worldwide employee engagement crisis.
Gallup Business Journal. Accessed at www.gallup.com/businessjournal/188033
/worldwide-employee-engagement-crisis.aspx?g_source=EMPLOYEE
_ENGAGEMENT&g_medium=topic&g_campaign=tiles on February 5, 2016.

Mann, A., & McCarville, B. (2016, January 19). Engaging employees: Big companies
need the most improvement. *Gallup Business Journal*. Accessed at www.gallup.com
/businessjournal/188675/engaging-employees-big-companies-need-improvement
.aspx?g_source=EMPLOYEE_ENGAGEMENT&g_medium=topic&g_campaign
=tiles on February 21, 2016.

Manzo, K. K. (2010, January 8). Whiteboards' impact on teaching seen as uneven.
Education Week, 3(2). Accessed at www.edweek.org/dd/articles/2010/01/08
/02whiteboards.h03.html?r=1701614447&preview=1 on March 30, 2015.

Marshall, K. (2014, January 2). *Teacher evaluation rubrics*. Accessed at www
.marshallmemo.com/articles/%20Teacher%20rubrics%20Jan%202014%20corr.pdf
on March 30, 2015.

Marzano, R. J., Waters, T., & McNulty, B. A. (2005). *School leadership that works:
From research to results*. Alexandria, VA: Association for Supervision and Curriculum
Development.

MetLife. (2013, February). *The MetLife survey of the American teacher: Challenges for
school leadership*. Accessed at www.metlife.com/assets/cao/foundation/MetLife
-Teacher-Survey-2012.pdf on April 1, 2015.

Mount, H. (2011, February 28). St. Paul's Cathedral anniversary: The beauty of the
domes that Wren built. *The Telegraph*. Accessed at www.telegraph.co.uk/culture/art
/architecture/8351434/St-Pauls-Cathedral-anniversary-the-beauty-of-the-domes
-that-Wren-built.html on February 4, 2016.

Mourshed, M., Chijioke, C., & Barber, M. (2010, November). *How the world's most
improved school systems keep getting better*. New York: McKinsey. Accessed at www
.mckinsey.com/client_service/social_sector/latest_thinking/worlds_most_improved
_schools on February 4, 2016.

New York City Department of Education (2015). *Advance guide for educators*. Accessed
at www.uft.org/files/attachments/advance-2015-16.pdf on February 4, 2016.

Newport, C. (2016). *Deep work: Rules for focused success in a distracted world*. New York: Hachette Book Group.

Pan, S. C. (2015, August 4). The interleaving effect: Mixing it up boosts learning. *Scientific American*. Accessed at www.scientificamerican.com/article/the-interleaving -effect-mixing-it-up-boosts-learning/ on February 4, 2016.

Peck, M. S. (1978). *The road less traveled: A new psychology of love, traditional values, and spiritual growth*. New York: Simon & Schuster.

Pfeffer, J. (2015). *Leadership BS: Fixing workplaces and careers one truth at a time*. New York: HarperCollins.

Porter, M. (1996, November-December). What is strategy? *Harvard Business Review*. Accessed at https://hbr.org/1996/11/what-is-strategy on February 4, 2016.

Porter, M. (2011). *On strategy*. Boston: Harvard Business School Press.

Reeves, D. (2002a). *The daily disciplines of leadership: How to improve student achievement, staff motivation, and personal organization*. San Francisco: Jossey-Bass.

Reeves, D. (2002b, May 8). Galileo's dilemma: The illusion of scientific certainty in educational research. *Education Week, 21*(34), 33, 44.

Reeves, D. (2006a). *Accountability in action: A blueprint for learning organizations*. Englewood, CO: Advanced Learning Press.

Reeves, D. (2006b). *The learning leader: How to focus school improvement for better results*. Alexandria, VA: Association for Supervision and Curriculum Development.

Reeves, D. (2008). *Reframing teacher leadership to improve your school*. Alexandria, VA: Association for Supervision and Curriculum Development.

Reeves, D. (2009a). *Assessing educational leaders: Evaluating performance for improved individual and organizational results* (2nd ed.). Thousand Oaks, CA: Corwin Press.

Reeves, D. (2009b). *Leading change in your school: How to conquer myths, build commitment, and get results*. Alexandria, VA: Association for Supervision and Curriculum Development.

Reeves, D. (2011). *Finding your leadership focus: What matters most for student results*. New York: Teachers College Press.

Reeves, D. (2012). The ketchup solution. *American School Board Journal, 199*(7), 35–36.

Reeves, D. (2015a). *The elements of grading* (2nd ed.). Bloomington, IN: Solution Tree Press.

Reeves, D. (2015b). *Inspiring creativity and innovation in K–12*. Bloomington, IN: Solution Tree Press.

Reeves, D. (2016). *FAST grading: A guide to implementing best practices*. Bloomington, IN: Solution Tree Press.

Riggs, L. (2013, October 18). Why do teachers quit? And why do they stay? *The Atlantic*. Accessed at www.theatlantic.com/education/print/2013/10/why-do -teachers-quit/280699 on March 24, 2015.

Santa Fe Community College. (n.d.) *Mission, vision, and core values.* Accessed at www .sfcc.edu/about_SFCC/our_mission on February 4, 2016.

Schmoker, M. J. (2011). *Focus: Elevating the essentials to radically improve student learning.* Alexandria, VA: Association for Supervision and Curriculum Development.

Shakespeare, W. (n.d.). *Julius Caesar.* Accessed at http://nfs.sparknotes.com/juliuscaesar /page_132.html on February 21, 2016.

Simon, D. A. (2012). Spaced and massed practice. In J. Hattie & E. M. Anderman (Eds.), *International guide to student achievement* (pp. 411–413). New York: Routledge.

Stiggins, R. (2007). Assessment through the student's eyes. *Educational Leadership, 64*(8), 22–26.

Strunk, W., Jr. (1918). *The elements of style.* Geneva, NY: Humphrey.

Thompson, A. (2007, May 11). *The blurry world of Claude Monet.* Accessed at www .livescience.com/1512-blurry-world-claude-monet-recreated.html on February 4, 2016.

Tomlinson, C. A. (2008). The goals of differentiation. *Educational Leadership, 66*(3), 26–31.

Top Nonprofits. (n.d.). *Fifty example mission statements.* Accessed at http://topnonprofits .com/examples/nonprofit-mission-statements on March 24, 2015.

Tough, P. (2012). *How children succeed: Grit, curiosity, and the hidden power of character.* Boston: Houghton Mifflin Harcourt.

Turner, S., & Ziebell, J. C. (2011). The career beliefs of inner-city adolescents. *Professional School Counseling, 15*(1), 1–14.

University of Oxford. (2002). *Oxford English dictionary* (5th ed.). Oxford, England: Oxford University Press.

Vatterott, C. (2010). Five hallmarks of good homework. *Educational Leadership, 68*(1), 10–15.

Weisinger, H., & Pawliw-Fry, J. P. (2015). *Performing under pressure: The science of doing your best when it matters most.* New York: Crown Business.

Western Australia Department of Education and Training. (n.d.). *Protocols for welcome to country and acknowledgement of traditional ownership.* Accessed at http:// generationone.org.au/uploads/assets/WelcomeToCountry.pdf on February 4, 2016.

Wiggins, A. (2014, October 10). *A veteran teacher turned coach shadows 2 students for 2 days—a sobering lesson learned.* Accessed at http://grantwiggins.wordpress.com/2014 /10/10/a-veteran-teacher-turned-coach-shadows-2-students-for-2-days-a-sobering -lesson-learned February 3, 2016.

Wiggins, G. (2015, March 30). *On reading part 5: A key flaw in using the Gradual Release of Responsibility model.* Accessed at http://grantwiggins.wordpress.com/2015 /03/30/on-reading-part-5-a-key-flaw-in-using-the-gradual-release-of-responsibility -model on March 30, 2015.

Yazzie-Mintz, E. (2010). Leading for engagement. *Principal Leadership, 10*(7), 54–58.

Zander, R. S., & Zander, B. (2000). *The art of possibility: Transforming professional and personal life*. Boston: Harvard Business School Press.

Zetlin, M. (2013, November 15). *The 9 worst mission statements of all time*. Accessed at www.inc.com/minda-zetlin/9-worst-mission-statements-all-time.html on March 24, 2015.

INDEX

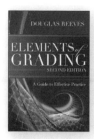

Elements of Grading, Second Edition
Douglas Reeves
The author provides educators with practical suggestions for making the grading process more fair, accurate, specific, and timely. In addition to examples and case studies, new content addresses how the Common Core State Standards and new technologies impact grading practices.
BKF648

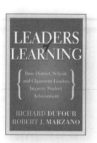

Leaders of Learning
Richard DuFour and Robert J. Marzano
Together, the authors focus on district leadership, principal leadership, and team leadership and address how individual teachers can be most effective in leading students—by learning with colleagues how to implement the most promising pedagogy in their classrooms.
BKF455

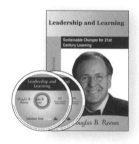

Leadership and Learning
Douglas Reeves
Everyone talks about the need for 21st century skills, but too many assessments are indistinguishable from those administered fifty to one hundred years ago. If educators want 21st century learning, they need 21st century assessment. Dr. Reeves suggests three fundamental shifts that must take place.
DVF049

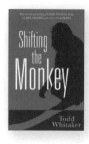

Shifting the Monkey
Todd Whitaker
Learn how to focus on your best employees first, and help them shift the "monkeys"—complaints, disruptions, and deflections—back to the underperformers. Through a simple and memorable metaphor, the author helps you reinvigorate your staff and transform your organization.
BKF612

Solution Tree | Press

a division of

Solution Tree

Visit SolutionTree.com or call 800.733.6786 to order.